Where Leads the Road

WILLIAM GORDON MALLETT

Where Leads the Road
Copyright © 2018 by William Gordon Mallett

All rights reserved. No part of this publication may be reproduced, distributed, or transmitted in any form or by any means, including photocopying, recording, or other electronic or mechanical methods, without the prior written permission of the author, except in the case of brief quotations embodied in critical reviews and certain other non-commercial uses permitted by copyright law.

Tellwell Talent
www.tellwell.ca

ISBN
978-0-2288-0184-9 (Hardcover)
978-0-2288-0183-2 (Paperback)
978-0-2288-0185-6 (eBook)

My Journey

My name is William (Bill) Gordon Mallett. I was born Nov.2nd 1944 on the island of Guernsey. I have one sister, Geraldene Sybil Adamson nee Mallett who was born Feb.13th 1943. Our father was William John Mallett who was born Dec.31st 1919 in Hamilton Ontario. Our mother was Sybil Ruth Mallett nee LeHuray who was born Mar.1st 1919 on the island of Guernsey.

Our paternal grandfather, William Arthur Mallett was born Aug.19th 1878 on the island of Guernsey. In 1913 he and his wife Marion Mallett nee Guy immigrated to Hamilton Ontario with their three daughters, Bertha, Anne, and Edna. While residing in Hamilton they had three more children, Gordon, Edith, and my father William (Bill).

In 1933 my grandfather decided to move back to Guernsey, taking my father and his older sister Edith with them. In 1939 the war began and when the Germans occupied the Channel Islands, my parents were trapped there. In December of 1941 they got married. After we were liberated we continued to live in the island. My father was a fisherman and I grew up around the harbour and fishing.

In 1954 my father moved the family to Hamilton Ontario, the place of his birth. The culture shock was hard, but at least we spoke the same language. Going to school and being laughed at because of my accent was rough at times. Constantly trying to fit in and be accepted as just one of the group. Wishing I was still at home in Guernsey where I did fit in.

As the years passed, things did get a lot easier. In 1962, at the time of the Cuban Missile Crisis, I joined the Canadian Navy and served for three years. It was a great experience and I learned a lot. It also instilled in me a sense of national pride. On my release from the Navy, I entered the Hamilton Fire Department and was there for forty years.

I got married to Aznive Saroyan born Jan. 2nd 1948 on Oct. 5th 1968. We are still together. On July 25th 1969 our first son William Melkon was born. Our second son Timothy Stephan was born Sept. 22nd 1971. Both are now married with children of their own.

I went back to Guernsey for a two week holiday in 1979. It cured any nostalgic wishing to return for ever. Guernsey is a beautiful island and a nice quiet place to live but it is no longer home. Canada is my home. The people and things I look back on from that time are gone. Time has moved on and with it has gone the place of my early youth. Now it is different and strange and Hamilton is where I fit in.

I am proud to be a Canadian and feel most blessed to live in this paradise. A land of opportunity and stability and peace. Nowhere else in the world can you find the combination we enjoy here. Anyone can be anything they want, all they have to do is reach out and grab it. With hard work, determination and drive you can accomplish anything you want. A lot of people seem to spend their time complaining about everything that is wrong instead of looking at everything that is right. The glass is half full, not half empty! If there is an injustice then do something positive to change it. Nothing is perfect, but if you think you have it bad, just try living in downtown Aleppo and see how you like it.

I have always loved history and poetry and read both extensively. There is a quote that says: "Those who do not learn from history, are doomed to repeat it." I truly believe that. Pierre Burton and Conrad Black are two writers that have explained Canada's history most eloquently. I wrote a poem about Canada and how lucky feel to be a Canadian.

Canada

On the anniversary of Canada's birth
I cast my mind on what it means to me
To be Canadian and all the worth
Of living in a land so free

I am not a Canadian by birth
I am a Canadian by choice you see
Of all the places on this earth
There is nowhere else I'd rather be

Land of forests, land of lakes
Land of mountains, land replete
Land of everything it takes
To make life happily complete

Home of chances for the taking
Opportunity beyond one's wildest dreams
Hope and success ready for the making
The answer to a dreamer's schemes

Everything you could ever need
Laid before you for the asking
All it takes is to do the deed
And reap the rewards of your tasking

I hear daily people groaning
Of the injustice, sad songs to sing
Instead of all the useless moaning
Do something positive to change these things

Look at things with a positive view
Every day is a brand new slate
Canada is a gift for you
Opportunity awaits you at the gate

On the news each day misery unfolds
Starving people, homeless refugees
Strife that makes the blood run cold
At the fate of those not as fortunate as we

So on this day and throughout the year
Be sure to give thanks and bless this land
Revel in the good fortune and hold dear
That which we each have in our hand

    I hope I have adequately stated my feelings for this marvellous country in which we live. May good fortune ever smile on Canada and give her peace. It was founded by daring adventurers who braved the wilderness and brought forth, whether by chance or good planning, a place that is as close to utopia as man in his imperfections could ever make. May that brave and entrepreneurial spirit carry us forward into the future.

This book is dedicated to my sister Geraldene Sybil Adamson nee Mallett, born Feb.13th 1943 and passed away November 30th 2017.

This poem was written by her when she was thirteen years old and was rediscovered when going through her belongings after her death.

Nature

Lightning streaks across the sky
Rending it in pieces
Wind and rain a-lashing by
Seems it never ceases
Waves come dashing up the beach
Heaving, restless, sighing
Then towards the early morn
Heavy winds are dying

Sunlight smiles into the east
The change from night to day
Since not worried in the least
Birds take their morning play
Thrushes, sparrows and the rest
Flying, swooping crying
Does your heart right good to see
Little birds are trying

Not a trace of storm is left
No clouds left in the sky
Spring heather in the cleft
Once wet, soon to be dry
Pink thrift blossoms sweet and fresh
Tall and crisp and cool
Blue waves have lost their whiteness
And look calm as a pool

Daisies lift a golden eye
As if to see the lark
Leave the earth and soar on high
Not to return 'til dark
No wee wind to stir the grass
So tall and green and lush
Some beauteous red roses
Give us a morning blush

With the passing of the day
The flower's heads now close
Twit'ring birds have ceased to play
The earth in darkness clothed
With the passing of the day
Last night is soon forgot
This is Mother Nature's way
Of proving fear means naught

Geraldene

At the close of day as descends the sun
Peace and tranquility spreads o'er the land
The turmoil and the bustle, struggles lost and won
Fade into the distance and are forgotten out of hand

So it is with life as we each fade into the past
Our troubles end and we find eternal rest
May the good that we did be the thing that lasts
And the memories we leave be of the best

Rest easy dear sister, and "Flights of
angels speed thee to thy rest"

Contents

CHAPTER 1: WHERE LEADS THE ROAD · 1

Where Leads the Road 2
Writer's Remorse 4
How Life Unfolds 6
Warming the Soul 8
Day's End 9
What It All Means 11
The Forests Wonder 12
Meandering Thoughts 13
Highway Hypnosis 15
Unknown Men of Valour 16
Little Man Syndrome 18
Fall in Woodlands Cemetery 20
A Bright New Day 21
Useful Platitudes 22
Senior's Moments 26
When You're Not There 27
By the Pool 28
Art for Art's Sake 29
Around the Bay 30
An Untold Story 31
The Cemetery 32
2016 33
2016 (Part Two) 35
2017 (The Saga Continues) 36
Mother's Day 38
Nature's Lessons 40
Symbiosis 41
Smoke and Mirrors 42
Enlightenment 44
Unfinished Symphony 45
Bastille Day in Nice 46
Her Majesty 47
The Demise of the English language 49
Life's Rewards 50
December 51
March 17th 52
Old Hulks 53
A Moment's Kindness 54
A Century Ago 55
Life's Cabaret 56
Hopes for Tomorrow 57
Dictatorial Dogma 58
Vive La Difference 59
Tomorrow 60
A Living Dream 61
One Night Stand 62
My Heart's Desire 64
Impulses 65
Anniversaries 66
Joy to the World 67

CHAPTER 2: TIME IN A NUTSHELL • 69

Time in a Nutshell 70
The Good Fight 73
Joey and Macy 74
Futurism 75
Acceptance 76
Aquatic Addiction 79
Your Legacy 80
You Reap What You Sow 81
Unwanted Changes 82
Tropical Time Frame 83
To Serve and Protect 84
'Tis the Season 85
Through the Tough Times 86
The Tides of life 87
The Panoply of Life 88
Thoughts of Love 89
The "Or Else" Factor 90
The Not So Shiny Prize 91
The Kiss of Elpis 92
The Religion of Love 93
Oceanus 94
Dark of the Moon 95
Changing of the Guard 97
The Loving Cup 98
Starts the Day 99

Letting Go 100
Summer's Bliss 101
Elysian Fields 102
Elpis Versus Moros 103
Civic Insanity 104
Souls Entwined 106
Ease the Moment 107
Joy in Life 108
Insomnia 110
She is My Gift 111
Finality 112
Imaginings 113
Happenstance 114
Defeating Consternation 115
Good Deeds 116
Reunited 117
Quiet Moments 118
Geriatrocity 119
Futile Hopes 120
From the Back Seat 121
Mall Watching 122
Life at Sea 123
K'ung Fu Tzu 125
Order and Symmetry 128
Nirvana 129

CHAPTER 3: SANDS OF TIME · *131*

The Sands of Time 132
Precious Moments 133
The Barrier of Age 134
Passion's Moment 135
My Life 136
Surviving the Storm 137
Summer's Heat 138
Mihi Omnes 139
Ad Finem Vitae 140
Simple Pleasures 141
Canada 142
Love's Remedy 144
Urgent Care 145
Zero I.Q. 146
Shifting Sands 148
Summer Enchantment 149
Self-Centered People 150
Love Refreshed 151
Relationships 152
Cemetery Sights 153
Ponderings 154
Love Is 156
Our Mortality 157
What's Next 158
Time's Passage 159
Love's Fair Favour 160
The Joy of Travel 161
R.I.P. 164
Life's Meaning 165
November 166
Life in a Hospital Gown 167
Banty Roosters 168
Authority Cruelly Used 169
Ad Nauseum 171
In the Afterglow 172
Personal Strength 173
Unbidden Things 174
Joie de Vivre 176
The Times of Janus 177
In Each Other 178
Egocentric Oafs 179
The First Day of the Rest of
Your Life 181
Ideal Fulfilled 182
Mandatory Attendance 183
Fulfillment 184
Internal Strife 185
A Winter Moment 188
Darwinism 189
Dealing with Life 191
Autumnal Equinox 192

CHAPTER 4: CONSEQUENCES · *193*

Consequences 194
Evening's Blessing 195
Hamilton Civic Cemeteries 196
Conflict from Confusion 199
Controlling Fate 200
Elocution of Love 201
A Breathing Space 202
Connections 203
Be Thankful for the Moment 204
Be My Valentine 205
Alternate Realities 206
June 6th, 1944 207
Unrealistic Views 210
Amor in Aeternum 211
Toxic People 212
Noel 213
New Year 214
Nature's Lesson 215
All That I desire 216
Move Ever Forward 217
All I Have to Give 218
May's Promise 219
Obsessive Compulsive 220
Canada at Vimy Ridge 221
Maintaining Calm 225
Loved Ones 226
Adoration 227
Looking Ahead 228
Life's Storms 229
Life to the Fullest 230
Leadership 231
It Matters not 232
Irrelevance 233
Inanity 234
In Order to Succeed 235
Impending End 236
Fanciful Fears 237
Equanimity 238
Emotions 239
Passage of Time 240
Old Age 241
Now is the Future 242
Religious Folly 243
Unknown Options 246
To Thine Own Self Be True 247
Time is the Cure 249
Time in Emergency 250
The Human Condition 251
The Great Leveller 252
Em Ge 253
Appreciation 254

CHAPTER 5: A FRESH START • 257

A Fresh Start **258**
Above and Beyond **259**
The Changing Seasons **260**
Second Childhood **261**
Random Thoughts **262**
Fantasy Land **263**
January 1ˢᵗ 2017 **264**
"What fools are we who cannot see The forest for the trees" **266**
The Future **267**
The Eternal Sea **268**
Democracy's Illusion **269**
A System Perpetuated **271**
Idealists **274**

The American Myth **277**
Thoughts on Life **280**
Philosophical Moments **281**
A Blank Page **282**
Demagoguery **284**
Not for Ourselves Alone **287**
Alternative Facts **289**
Revolution **291**
A Good Deeds Reward **293**
Subsumption **294**
Personal Priorities **295**
The Fading Light **296**
The Fullness of Life **297**

• CHAPTER ONE •
Where Leads the Road

Where Leads the Road

A child is born and a new journey starts
All is fresh and opportunities are rife
Everything that happens will play a part
In forming the future of this child's life

The warmth of a mother's loving arms
A father's strength to protect and provide
The assuredness of being safe from harm
Builds a child's confidence from inside

The child is a blank page on which fate will write
Each experience will leave its' mark
Good ones will move the child to the light
Bad ones will lead towards the dark

Each time the child comes to a fork on the way
Past history plays a part in the decision
Experience will dictate the mode and play
And colour the light of their vision

Hence, children who were raised in gentleness
Will tend to make their choices in kind
Those that were not so happily blessed
Shall choose with a more selfish mind

Nurture and nature both have a hand
In shaping the actions that we take
We don't notice when we decide on a stand
Things influencing the decisions that we make

The road of life is a convoluted thing
Hither and yon we are carried along
By outside influences which bring
Into play old experiences, right or wrong

What set our feet upon the path we took
What unseen forces influenced the way we went
What lines on the pages of our life's book
Dictated the outcome of our bent

Life is a mysterious ebb and flow
Influenced not by unknown, unseen powers
But by the events that happen as we grow
And circumstances hour by hour

Writer's Remorse

I have found, to my chagrin, a grim reality
That writing rhymes is not the hardest part
Rather the printing of my work has come to be
My bete noir and quite painful from the start.

I started out so full of excitement and hope
That my work would be in print for all to see
Imagining the criticisms with which I'd have to cope
Wishing it to be accepted by at least some willingly.

The first step was the editing and a few suggestions
As to how my verses should be presented and arranged
But when it came back, to my indignation,
My whole body of work had been rearranged.

My work was altered way beyond my recognition
Changing the words, rhymes and cadence and such
So that I could hardly recognize the compilation
Of the work in which I had invested so much.

The time between each step seemed interminably long
And I basically had to rewrite the whole thing to look
The way it did before they switched it out so wrong
Not at all the way I had originally planned my book.

The cover that their designer picked, was very bland
And I finally picked one that I thought fit the theme
At least that part was quite easy out of hand
Fitting in quite nicely in my scheme.

Another rather sore point is the way
I had to pay extra to edit the changes they selected
If they had left things how I wrote them originally
I would not have needed to get them all corrected.

Unfortunately, as an unknown untried beginner
I must use the companies that offer up self-publish
Once a writer is an established winner
You can pick and choose who, where and how to finish.

How Life Unfolds

In November of 1960 my working life began
It was a shock, to say the least, everything so new
I moved out of childhood into the age of man
Not knowing what was expected of me or what I had to do

Traumatic and exciting, wanting to know everything
The harshness of the working world, no gentleness at all
Eager and afraid of what each new day would bring
Everybody waiting to jump on your next trip and fall

Being the butt end of jokes with no quarter given
The rights of passage were quite tough, but in the end
Learning not to show how bad your feelings had been riven
Hardened up your will and thus paid dividends

Moving from job to job, trying to find success
A stint in Canada's Navy gave me a broader view
Travelling far and wide, being foolish, young and restless
Surviving many rash things that uncouth youth will do

Returning to civilian life brought another batch
Of culture shock, an adjustment to the world out there
Looking for employment and trying to find a match
For my brief but varied talents that I had to share

The Fire Department was recruiting, so I took a chance
Thinking it would do until I could find a new career
Time passed and my interest took another stance
I found that this was where I wanted to spend my working years

Through forty plus years I rode the rigs to countless alarms
Some amazing disastrous things that defy imagination
It was very satisfying to ease the victim's harm
And help be the one who could alleviate the situation

The people that I worked with and the people on the street
All of the events, both the great and small
The excitement and the adrenalin rush made the job replete
With a satisfaction that held you in it's thrall

Finally the powers that be said that it was time to go
And they sidelined me to cemeteries where I passed the time
Burying the dead and maintaining all the grow
Around the grounds and graves in all types of climes

The kaleidoscope of people was another education
Both the workers and the visitors to the grounds
In people's response to death there is great variation
Everything from silence to a cacophony of sound

Now, at last I have come to that point in the road
I am no longer a part of the working world day to day
It can be intimidating, not knowing what the future holds
After a lifetime of having such a regulated way

But I am still the master of what the future has to give
So I shall have to map, personally, the way to go
"Use it or lose it" is the credo by which I will live
And look to the new career which in time will grow

Warming the Soul

When love touches you thus
It forever will be
All your life's focus
Your soul running free
Awaiting the bliss
Of your loved one's kiss.

The touch of the hand
And the heart skips a beat
A feeling so grand
The soul is replete
Love is the expression of heaven on earth
Complete and entire, a whole person's worth.

Day's End

The time I like the best
Is as the sun sinks in the west
And the stress and bustle of the day is over in the main
After all is said and done
Seeking out the one
Who makes my life whole and eases all my pain.

To sit quietly beside
My love, slowly letting slide
Every knot and wrinkle of the day
To reach out and gently touch
Her soft skin means so much
All the vexations just seem to melt away.

As we silent sit a moment
All the bustle and the foment,
Of daily troubles are banished to a distant part,
While no words need be spoken
The tensions drift and are broken
As warmth between us heals every scar.

With brushing finger tips
And eager seeking lips
The troubles and the world just fade away
As the passion rises
To an exploding crisis
Lightning bolts of pleasure save the day.

Now that the moment has waned
And reality has gained
A foothold as you lay entwined
With your battery recharged
You can face the world at large
And peace will surely fill the mind.

To have someone who
Can fill your life for you
Is the greatest gift you can receive
Bless the day you found
Each other and be bound
Together for all eternity.

What It All Means

As the clock ticks down to zero and the sands are running out
In the hour glass of a loved one close to death
Your mind slips into turmoil and starts to cast about
For the reason or the point that lies beneath.

Life at times seems pointless and what does it all mean
Are we just dust in the Fates wind floating free
Is it all just random chance or what message can we glean
From the passing of the one we loved so dear.

Perhaps the truth lies in what we leave behind
Does the good outweigh the bad in our travails and woes
May the legacy be building blocks for the future to find
So our passing this way will have helped to ease the flow.

The Forests Wonder

Deep in the midst of the forest's stand
Where the height of the trees blocks the sun
The occasional ray breaking through to the land
The arching branches form a vaulted roof
Giving the feeling of a cathedral grand
A quasi-religious experience filling you
The sense of nature so near at hand

The solitude of the natural space
The sounds of the birds and animals there
The absence of intrusion into the place
By bustling people and the world
To disturb the moment of unsullied grace
A fulfilling sensation to be savoured
The blessing of life falling across your face.

Meandering Thoughts

As I sit and listen
To the hardening of my arteries
Random thoughts on life and truth
Spring unbidden in the mind
All the things that have occurred
That brought me to this place and time
Things I have seen and people that I've met
Events that changed the path that my feet trod

How happenstance creates randomly the order of things
The butterfly flaps it's wings in Tokyo
Causing a tornado in Kansas
An unknown radical named Princip
Set forth the holocaust of World War One

How some people can get others to do their bidding
Because they want to
While others must rely on brute authority

Everyone's inability to see themselves as others see them
People with such inadequacy complexes
That they overcompensate with outsized egos
Those with low IQs trying to prove how smart they are
When all they do is prove the opposite

How each person responds to extreme stimulus
Such as danger, fear, sorrow, disaster
Why some rise to the occasion
While others fold under pressure

The way in which triumph or disaster is faced
Both are fleeting and transitory

Why some rely on others for support
And others face their daily struggle alone and unaided

We each of us deal with things in our own way
We are forced to play the cards we're dealt
Random chance deals the cards
How we respond is our own choice

Highway Hypnosis

Driving down the tunnel of my headlights in the dark
Seeing nothing outside the light's limiting play
The dots on the roadway are the only mark
To show the passing of the miles along your way

It seems to parallel the scope of our world
So bound in by our needs and our context
We rarely step aside as time unfurls
To look beyond the horizon and what's next

Time passes by unnoticed as the years slip away
And we are focused on the most immediate
On and on, so ticks the clock and counts the days
Until at last we're standing at death's gate
Leaving all that we have not said or done
Unfinished, left with victories unwon

Strike now, the hour is drawing nigh
Squeeze every last drop until the well is dry

Unknown Men of Valour

How great would it be
To be a part of history
To be there on the day the whole world changed
At Dien Bien Phu
Or at Waterloo
Takes the breath away as things were rearranged

I wonder on the men
Who were there when
The face of history was altered in a day
They who faced the fury
Of the battle not the glory
That came after when the smoke had cleared away

The generals all get fame
From the war's bloody game
And politicians pass out awards for the foray
But the grunt down at the bottom
Will quickly be forgotten
Even though it was him that saved the day.

The private that never broke
Under the sabre's stroke
Who stayed the tide and turned the cavalry away
Who planted and firmly stood
Where it would do the most good
Is forgotten when history recalls the day.

Still in that soldiers heart
Is the knowledge of the part
That he and his mates stood firm when others fled
As brothers they were one
And when the deed was done
Their pride will stand long after they are dead.

The best award that's won
Is the one that goes unsung
Except by those who shouldered the barrage
The pride when you meet
One of your brothers on the street
Each knowing the other's bravery and courage.

The next time that you see
A soldier's cross try to be
A little thoughtful of the price that these men paid
On the day of the battle's crest
They stayed firm and passed the test
And deserve an honoured place in our history.

Little Man Syndrome

There are people in this world with phobias
About their own perceptions of themselves
And what they see as their inadequacies

In small men this often manifests itself
In an over inflated ego out of all proportion
To their true size and capabilities

You see these strutting little martinets
Parading around trying to show how good they are
My father used to say:
"If you have to tell people how good you are
Chances are you ain't"
Let your actions speak for themselves

God forbid that these individuals should ever
Reach a position of authority
Because they become tyrannical
Since fear of their inadequacies drives them
To rule by force rather than by favour

Leadership comes from within
Not from the force of a club
The harder they push
The more self-defeating they become
The rest of the world look at these puffed up banty roosters
And laugh at their antics and overblown ego
Banty roosters simply do not have the ability
To see how they are perceived by the world at large
Hence they exist in their own little world
Where they are God and all else is secondary

Robert Burns said:

"WOULD THAT GOD THE SENSE HAD GI'E US TO SEE OURSELVES AS OTHERS SEE US"

They are truly little, little people

Fall in Woodlands Cemetery

Late October and the rains have begun
Cold and wet and dripping down the stones
The leaves are coating the ground in death
All is sadness around with the songs unsung
Here amidst the moldering bones
Frost will soon come and place a white wreath
Across the scene with tranquility
Fall is the season of cemeteries.

A Bright New Day

The sun is up and bright the day
Banishing the darkness of the night
All is hope and warmth along the way
Toward the future, looking bright
Each day is a brand new slate
To start toward the future's gate.

Useful Platitudes

Don't kill
Don't steal
Don't lie
Don't cheat
Are all rules that can't be beat

Try turning the other cheek
The earth inherited by the meek

Do unto others as you would
Have them do for you if you could

Many times you have heard them say
Save your strength for another day

All work and no play
Makes Jack a boy who's dull and gray

A stitch in time will stop the fray
Sparing further damage along the way

Be sure your sins will find you out
Is often true without a doubt

Truth carries the biggest clout
No matter how loud the lies may shout
Every dog has its day
Hence be careful how you play

When you wish, do so with care
It may come back to singe your hair

Be nice to others and you will find
It will come back to you in kind

You will find that a job begun
Is a job that's halfway done

The journey of a thousand miles
Starts with one step and a smile

If you have an elephant to eat
Take small bites, or else you're beat

Respect is a thing that's earned, not given
To each of us no matter how driven

Respect for elders is a must
Lest all your labours come to dust

What goes around comes back to you
Hence be good in what you do
(Pay back is a bitch)

No matter the riches you accumulate
You can't take it with you through death's gate

Time heals all wounds for you
But time wounds all heels is also true

When skinning a cat there's more than one way
To accomplish the deed despite what they say

Many a good tune played on an old fiddle
Is a very useful riddle

Youth is wasted on the young
It's over almost before it's begun

Goodness is its own reward
Even when there's no regard

Gather ye rosebuds while ye may
For tomorrow is another day

Many's the slip 'twixt cup and lip

Once milk is spilled, shed no tears
Mop it up and move on to what appears

Children say the darndest things
Amazing in the truth they bring

In youth all is black and white
The older you get, more gray your sight

The longer you live, the faster time goes
Inexorably onward to the future it flows

The farther up the tree the monkey ascends
The more exposed becomes his posterior's end

Be nice to those you pass on the up escalator
As you will see them on the down bound later

As the sapling, so the maple
Is a truth that is a staple

The cup of revenge promises much
But gives nothing with it's touch

He who points his finger in blame
Has three pointing at self for shame

The one thing riches cannot buy
Is time no matter what you try

Compassion and kindness are much better
Than following the law to the letter

There's always the exception that proves the rule
Should be obvious to all, except a fool
An empty barrel makes a loud noise you'll find
Is especially true of an empty mind

"Shoemaker look to your shoes"
Also applies to me and you

Physician heal thyself is a good idea
Don't wait for others to give the panacea

He who cries wolf will discover soon
The result of singing a well-worn tune

No one's memory is that strong
To be a good liar for very long

"Don't care" comes to a bad end will always be
Proved in the end by posterity

There are hundreds more out there
Feel free to add your own

Senior's Moments

In a senior's moment, when boredom filters in
As I sit and contemplate on how my life has been
I marvel at the speed with which it all went by
And feel some mild regret at the things I did not try.

Wondering about "the path not taken"
How would my world have been shaken
By putting my foot on that other path
What difference from what I now hath.

'Tis but a momentary slip into fanciful meanderings
On missed opportunities, capriciously pandering
To fantasies imagined about things not done
Or challenges not met that could have been won.

Then the moment passes and reality sets in
That's when warm memories start to begin
Making me feel glad about the path I did take
To where I am now, a success, not a mistake.

When You're Not There

At times in the day when things are slow
And time hangs heavy on my hands
I think of when we are together and how
Life is much brighter, not so bland
Time without you is no delight
When I'm with you, you fill the night.

By the Pool

Sitting quietly on the upper deck by the pool
Awaiting the giant cruise ship's getting under way
Not yet knowing who is loud and who is cool
But it won't be long before the characters display

You'll get the strutters and the preeners
The arrogant and the keeners
The thinkers and the coasters
The intelligent and the boasters
The veterans and the new
The timid and the shrewd

A cross section of life, all within your reach
Lessons freely given that no school could ever teach

Art for Art's Sake

Beauty is in the beholder's eye they say
But I don't believe this is totally true
Since some of the art that is presented today
Is really not what I'd consider good.

If someone has to explain to you
What it is that you are looking at now
To me that says that it's less than good
Just another pretentious show

It's "the Emperor's new clothes" anew
Everyone is afraid to voice
That the piece that is now on view
Is less than stellar, not my choice

Afraid that they will look quite crass
Uneducated, tasteless, unrefined
Definitely not of the class
Of art lovers, so defined.

"Oh, the colours are so well planned"
"The brush strokes, ah what technique"
"The subject matter is quite grand"
"The styling is so unique"

All euphemisms for what a load
Of talentless art that could be done
By an eight year old with crayons
In an art class in grade one.
(Stay inside the lines)

Around the Bay

The starting line is crowded with hundreds eager to be away
Excitement mounting as the start draws near
Adrenalin is pouring, and the nerves are frayed
Till finally the starting horn rings out in their ears

And so begins the ordeal of the 32 kay annual race
Around Burlington Bay it makes its winding weft
The first half flat as a pancake encourages a quicker pace
The last third a rollercoaster to sap out whatever's left

The gazelles at the front soon leave the field in the dust
Next comes the wannabes trying to keep pace
In the middle ride the bulk of the field who just
Want to do a personal best on this particular day

The ones I think that deserve the most credit are
The poor sad sack limpers who drag in the back
They don't quit and work the hardest by far
No one's there to see them as they complete their track

That last poor dude who crosses the line when the rest are done
With blistered feet and aching joints, absolutely drubbed
Should get a medal for completing the run
Congratulations brother, you're a member of the club!

An Untold Story

The indigent sits in a doorway full of sorrow
Sad eyed, begging for your change
Dirty, smelly, with no hope for the morrow
Hoping for enough for him to exchange
For something that will make him feel good
For a moment, dope, alcohol, or a little food

Yesterday did not at all go right
His cadging efforts came to next to naught
Cold and hungry with no relief in sight
Hoping for an escape from where he's caught
In a downward spiral to the end
With alcohol or drugs his only friend

The odds are that he will meet his end
Alone in some back alley out of sight
A victim of his life's destructive trend
There's no saving grace at all in his plight
He made bad choices and now there's no way back
Only a pauper's grave at the end of the track

If only one could turn back to a time
Before this lifestyle was etched in stone
To when he was still in his prime
Turning his feet from the path he chose
Letting him be something other than
A broken, empty, useless shell of a man

Ah, would that it were ever so
But sadly, that's just not how it goes

The Cemetery

And in that place where loved ones mourn,
Amid the resting souls,
And muted sounds drift softly down
Between the blocks of stone.

Here where life's strife and trouble end.
Death comes to ease the pains
Dear ones come to pay respects
To the departed's last remains.

Some find peace and solace here,
Some feel guilt or loss,
Some feel warmth in the memories glow
Of times shared with those who've crossed.

Time rolls on in endless waves,
The seasons ceaseless varying
The silent sentinels of the graves
Remain to mark their passing.

2016

In a few more days in the You Ess of Ay
The people will go to the polls
This election has been almost obscene
In the approach that the candidates extoll

Hillary no doubt has been questionable about
Her connections to Wall Street and power
While Donald will try to sell any lie
To arouse the audience's attention that hour

No one votes for who they want to win through
They go out against the one they hate
The voters should see (between you and me)
The truth before it's too late

Both candidates are not shining stars
They are quite sketchy at best
But thinking a bit will show the truth of it
And prove who should pass the test

Just think of Trump as a cancerous lump
Which is terminal and the patient will die
While Clinton, it's true, is like a bad flu
But will pass and the patient survive

Logic should really dictate the future that awaits
After the election is all said and done
That no matter who will manage to squeak through
They too shall pass and be gone

> "THE TUMULT AND THE SHOUTING DIES THE CAPTAINS AND THE KINGS DEPART"
>
> *Recessional by Rudyard Kipling*

2016 (Part Two)

The worst has happened in the You Ess of Ay
Donald Trump has been elected to the Presidency
Now the biggest huckster of them all will hold sway
Over the richest, most indebted nation in the world you see

The greatest snake oil salesman of them all
Has conned the great unwashed that he's the one
With this much power he can fleece them all
In thanks for all that they have done

One other person convinced a nation
That he was the saviour of the day
When he was finished to much consternation
Europe was in ruins, his country laid waste

Let us hope that this is not the case here
And sanity will take hold before it's too late
But given past history it's hard not to fear
The worst case scenario is at our gate

History will record the events that take place
We can't see the future (if only we could)
So be optimistic, put on a good face
Maybe it will all turn out to the good

2017
(The Saga Continues)

We are now on to day three
Of Donald Trump's presidency
He did not disappoint his detractors
He's totally focused on
Being THE number one
Ignoring all other factors.

In true Trump fashion
He's showed that his passion
Is completely just Me, Me, Me
Trying to show he's so great
And when anyone baits
He lashes out with venom and glee

His reactions are wild
Like a petulant child
To anything that is said to detract
From his inane bleating
And endless tweeting
And twisting the truth and the facts

It would appear to us all
That he's fumbling the ball
Ego causing him to unravel
The scary part
That should grip at your heart
Is he's in charge of a nuclear arsenal

This is only day three
So what folly we'll see
In the future is hard to discern
But I truly believe
All he's got up his sleeve
Is ad lib and that's cause for concern

I wonder how long
Before it goes really wrong
And they decide it was a mistake
This narcissistic man
Who lacks any plan
Was just a charlatan, a grandiose fake

Pray for the day
When they take him away
In a straight jacket. raving incoherently
Let's hope it's before
He's started a war
Having damaged things irreparably

Mother's Day

The most unconditional love of all
Is the love of a mother for her child
It will risk anything, answer any call
No matter where or what or how wild
For the need she will give her all.

To her last breath she will always be
The one you can go to when all else fails
She will side with you unquestioningly
Doing her best to get you back on the rails
Over your troubles and fancy free.

Mothers are seldom given enough appreciation
Or credit for all they do for you
They've been there no matter what the situation
Or how hard things are, they will always do
Whatever they can to aid in a solution.

Once they are gone and it's too late
To say all the things we should have said
We realize what we had, now fate
Has taken her to the land of the dead
Leading her through that one-way gate.

On this day in May, once a year
Take the time to think about
Your mother and how dear
She is, and without a doubt
Her true worth will become quite clear.

Do what you can to show her how
Much you appreciate all she's done for you
Give her the respect she's due and with a bow
Thank her for everything and seeing you through
To the success you have achieved up to now.

Nature's Lessons

The gentle kissing of wavelets on the sand
A slow soft onshore breeze on the blow
The warmth of the sun beaming down on the land
All combining together to make the heart glow.
Ah, would that this moment could last forever
Perpetually onward, ceasing never.

Life by the sea is a marvellous thing
Whether summer or winter or autumn or spring
Each season with wonders that they will bring
The might of the gale, the howl of the storm
Picking up pieces of detritus the next morn
Stoic determination with which it is borne.

Symbiosis

Management and labour are a contentious mess
Constantly feuding in a perpetual melee
Labour always wants to be paid more for doing less
While management wants labour to do more for free

Without the company the worker's job would not be
Without the worker the company would fold
They each need the other, it is plain to see
Two sides of the same coin when all is told

A fair day's work for a fair day's pay should be the rule
Conversely a profit must be made for the company
One hand washes the other, each adding to the pool
For the common good of all to go forward happily

Mutual trust and respect is needed for success
An honest effort on both sides, a win for all aboard
Since each has a stake in it, it is for the best
For everyone to share equally in the outcome and rewards

"All for one and one for all" is imperative
For success to follow on the tail
Of the toil and effort of the mutual collective
All contributing their share for the common weal

Smoke and Mirrors

The wings of the mind spread far and wide
Carrying us to new and unimagined heights
Contemplating the unknown from every side
Bringing forth great truths into sight

There are those who would obscure the facts
Stating things that are blatantly wrong
Undeterred by the truth it is their tack
To make their fables loud and strong

Rewriting history to suit their needs
Stating it long and hard and fast to sway
People, distracting from the actual deeds
Counting on flash and glitz to win the day

Many are convinced by the carnival show
Confused by the hand being quicker than the eye
But sooner or later the cover will be blown
The truth will out no matter what they try

There is a Chinese proverb that says:

"FROM HE WHO TRULY SEEKS, THE TRUTH WILL NOT LONG REMAIN HIDDEN"

Enlightenment

Ignorance is a large dark void without any light
Knowledge is like a candle shining so bright
Each candle that is lit helps improve our sight
Adding to the collective dispelling of the night

We each of us contribute to the betterment of all
By igniting our own candle to add to the light
Passing on the torch to the next one in the hall
Making brightness greater and improving our plight

Prejudice and ignorance lead to fear and aggression
That which we do not understand we fear
The spread of knowledge and facts helps relieve the tension
Bringing calm and making the situation more clear

Tyrants always fan the flames of hate and ignorance
Giving the masses somewhere for their anger to focus
The "them and us" mentality will inevitably spread intolerance
Accelerated by the rhetoric and obfuscating hocus pocus

Don't let the dark of ignorance overwhelm your light
Protect your candle from the winds of hate
Let logic and knowledge keep it burning bright
Illuminating and forcing the dark to dissipate

Go forth in amity and instead of aggression
Light your candle and thrust it forth instead
The light you spread will help to dampen hatred's passion
Don't cure the headache by cutting off the head

Unfinished Symphony

The long hall of life echoes with the footsteps of the past
The light of the present, into the future does not shine
The speed with which it all goes by is so incredibly fast
In the blinking of an eye a year has gone down the line

One is left breathless, it seems you're barely in your prime
Then suddenly you're old and gray and life has flown by
All that is left are memories, snapshots out of time
To warm the coldness of old age and keep you feeling spry

Make the most of each moment that you have every day
No one can tell how much time you have left to spend
Live life to the fullest, don't let anything delay
The band is playing and who knows when the music ends

Bastille Day in Nice

The sun comes up on a warm summer day
The birds are singing and all seems well
'til the news breaks and sad to say
Yet another terrorist attack to tell
The people of France struck yet again
Numerous deaths and suffering and pain.

A mad man struck on Bastille Day
In Nice on the boardwalk by the beach
Driving a truck through people at play
Masses of people within his reach
Until finally the police gunned him down
Ending the mayhem he had sown.

May his soul forever in hell burn
Next to the others of his kind
These days it is all too common a turn
The frequency really boggles the mind
The suffering he caused will not soon ease
Would that the victims will find peace.

In the world today to me it seems
That madness and mayhem rule the day
My hope is that sanity will hold sway
But I fear that that is but a dream
Let peace and love conquer and cease the fall
Lest the maelstrom consumes us all.

Her Majesty

On the ninetieth anniversary of her birth
There is no one who is more deserving
Or has better proved her worth
Than the woman who is now serving
As our monarch and the reigning queen
Through the trials and tribulations that she has seen.

The title of "Her Majesty" is one that truly fits
She is a paragon of all the admirable attributes
She moves with grace and the Royal Mantle sits
Well upon her shoulders and the crown suits
Her well, she has been a hallmark for us all
A standard for us to rise to, well above the pall.

She has led her life in duty and steadfastness
Through wars and scandals and upheaval's thrust
Governments come and go but she is there to bless
Us with a constancy that we've come to trust
If we could all live our lives as well as she
What a better place to live in this world would be.

William Shakespeare said:

"A SCEPTRED MONARCH BETTER THAN HIS THRONE"

The Demise of the English language

Once the English language was a musical thing
In the flower of the words and the turn of a phrase
Now the gutter rules and expediency brings
The end of grammar and thoughts that amaze

Instead of "Good morning" now it's "Yo"
No longer "How are you", "Wazzup" is the norm
Profanity is acceptable in the to and fro
Slang is now the benchmark of form

Instead of raising the standards higher
And teaching the language as it should be
We are degenerating down in the mire
And accepting things as expediency

Soon the language of the Bard will be gone
Dead as Latin and Greek of old
Prose as we know it will be done
And the beauty of poetry covered in mold

One cannot turn back the sands of time
Once the genie is out, there's no going back
The flower of literature and of rhyme
Will live only in memory, fading to black.

Life's Rewards

The road of life stretches into the fog of time
Undulating forward into the unknown
Presaging hope and sunnier climes
Reaping the fruit of the seeds we've sown
The past will come back into play
Old mistakes catching up from behind
Hence, whatever you do today
Will come back to you in kind.
We tend to do what's expedient
Rather than what is truly right
If we can for a moment relent
Our haste and need and endless flight
For the pot of gold at the rainbow's end
It will pay in the future, dividends

December

How cold the ground, how grey the sky
Before the wind the dead leaves fly
The skeletal branches skyward plead
In hopes of catching the sun's scant heat.

The days are short, the nights are long
Not soon to hear the first robin's song
The snow is crisp, the hoarfrost spreads
Relentless across the window ledge.

The snow falls silent to the earth
Blanketing all in a wonderous girth,
Making everything silent and sterile
Dazzlingly beautiful for a while.

Children building with the snow,
Forts and sculptures all aglow
White missiles flying back and forth
Sounds of laughter, joy and mirth.

It seems that in the midst of winter's thrall
The snow brings the child out in us all
People love to skate and sled or ski
And rush to do it gleefully.

And so when autumn is so drear,
Just remember winter's near
Cold snowy days so crisp and clear
Then soon to follow, spring is here.

March 17th

St. Patrick's Day is here once again
And all the world turns green for a day
"Kiss me I'm Irish" is in the main
And Irish Folk Music overrides the sway.

"May the wind be always at your back,
May the road rise up to greet you,
May a light rain fall softly on your shoulders,
May the sun shine forever on your face,
And may you be in heaven ten minutes
before the Devil knows you're dead."

An old Irish proverb

Old Hulks

At the far end of the harbour lies the graveyard of ships
The old ones that no longer ply their trade
They lay there rusticating waiting for that final trip
Into the melting pot where razor blades are made

They are old and tired, their paint is faded and peeling
They'll never point their bows to the seas' open arms
Their day is done and there is an overriding feeling
Of sadness for past days full of glory and of charm

So it is with people as time erodes youth's spring
Gray hair and the weight of years shall bend the back
The furrows and creases on the face that age will bring
Too soon appear with the years' ceaseless track
Enjoy the time you have while you still may
Who knows what comes with the dawning of the day

A Moment's Kindness

The sun is shining and the birds are singing
The bustle of life moves forward
But for some struggle is a constant thing
Stretching to the horizon forever onward
Not for all a place in the sun
For some each day is never fun

If we could each spare a moments grace
A touch of kindness, so small a thing
Smoothing the lines on someone's face
Giving a bit of hope on which to cling
From those of us that have so much
Giving to someone a warming touch

It costs you so little so to grace
A gift to them, no loss to you really
You will not notice any absence
Of what you choose to give so freely
But your life will be improved
By the bit of suffering you've removed

A Century Ago

On Vimy Ridge, a place in France
There stands a monument, names to tell
Forever marking in remembrance
Where thirty-six hundred Canadians fell

Seven thousand more were wounded there
Four thousand with a fate unknown
They fought with bravery beyond compare
They gave their all and gained renown

It was the deed no one else could do
But Canada stepped up and took the chore
Showing to all Canada could win through
A strong young nation coming to the fore

The cost was high, the price was dear
But those young men did not shrink
They came forward without fear
Into shot and shell, they did not blink

On this the Centennial of that deed
Let us remember well those men
Who gave their all when there was need
We shall not see their like again

Life's Cabaret

The stage is set and ready to go
All that is needed is the star of the show
Enter stage left, the production's begun
Time for your moment in the sun

Life is a play with many acts and scenes
Full of plans and hopes and dreams
The curtain goes up the performance begun
Never stopping 'til the star's time has run

Make sure your star shines with a burning light
Dispelling the darkness of the night
Use what time you have to do all that you might
Before the curtain comes down and you fade from sight.

Hopes for Tomorrow

On her father's arm the bride walks down the aisle
All eyes turn to watch her slow progression
The groom waits at the altar with a nervous smile
The organ plays soft music for the long procession

Once the altar is reached the father leaves the bride
Signalling the end of this phase of her life
Together they turn to face the priest side by side
To exchange their vows and become husband and wife

Now is the time of nostalgia and hope for tomorrow
Childhood is left behind with sadness in the heart
The vows are spoken softly with a hint of sorrow
Underlying the excitement of the brand new start

The ceremony complete with joined hands they now proceed
Greeting their guests and friends at the reception hall
And, as one, they now begin to lead
Their life as a couple with all it's joys and squalls

May the happiness encompassing them never fade
May fortune smile upon them ever so
May success be present in the life they've made
May peace and contentment pave their future road

Dictatorial Dogma

Ra is setting in the western sky
While Osiris, being crucified
Prays to Buddha, who sits and smiles
At Ganesha and his elephant wiles.

The Golden Calf rises and falls
The Ten Commandments are writ on the walls
Novenas are prayed to Mary's grace
Belief is etched on every face.

Don't shave your beard, you must cover your face
Wrap your head in a rag or be disgraced
Jehovah is whispering in Joseph Smith's ear
Just follow the rules, there's nothing to fear.

Don't kill, don't steal, don't lie, don't cheat
Are definitely rules that can't be beat
But thinking that yours is the one true way
Is a folly that defies all logical sway.

Killing someone who's not of your belief
Is absolute insanity without relief
Then claiming the religion is of peaceful intent
Makes one marvel at how the words are bent.

God lives not in the Promised land
Nor in the dogma of one man's hand
By living a life that is true and straight
Is actually the way to heaven's gate.

Vive La Difference

Men and women are melded to perfection
They are designed to do different things
These roles came through natural selection
And are the culmination that success will bring
This does not make them necessarily unequal
Nor should it give them contentious roles
Rather it makes both of them a sequel
Of each other to make up the whole.

The trend today seems to be a blurring of the lines
Between the male and female and I cannot define
Why one would want to be like the other when
I love the difference 'twixt women and men
The great beauty of life I always find
To reside in the female form divine
To be like them is not my wish
I'd rather worship them with a kiss.

If things keep progressing in this trend
Humanity will become an amorphous mass
With no distinction between each gender
Completely bland, how very crass.
And so I say "Vive la difference"
Let each be what they were meant to be
May there always be a divergence
Of the line between "he and she".

Tomorrow

As the days dwindle down and retirement looms
I sit and cast my eyes around the lunch room
Looking at the group of which I am presently a part
Wondering what it will be like after I depart

I have been working for fifty-six years
The future is unknown territory I fear
I must look forward with hope in my heart
Enjoying the newness of a fresh start

Nowhere I have to be this day
Just meandering time along the way
Life must have a purpose, an aim, an intent
Without which ambition's drive is spent

Use it or lose it is my creed
Hence, I must create a need
So I shall have to fill my time
Recording life's events in rhyme

A Living Dream

Her smile lights up the room like sunshine
Her eyes are dark alluring pools mysterious
She moves with grace and ease sublime
Her lips hold promises delirious
That she is mine is beyond all measure
Her love is truly my life's treasure

One Night Stand

Ardor fades and passion cools
Leaving a void that must be filled
The warmth of love should be the rule
Not indifference once the lust is stilled
The tenderness of a warm embrace
Will put a smile on your lover's face

Too often once the hot flash is past
There lacks the personal interaction
There is no building of a love that lasts
When all that started it was physical attraction
Love is a flower that must be groomed
If you want it to continue to bloom

Lao Tzu said:

"MARRIAGE IS THREE PARTS LOVE AND SEVEN PARTS FORGIVENESS"

My Heart's Desire

When things get slow, and there's little about
My thoughts drift to my love so dear
Wishing I was with her without a doubt
To pay lip service to her so near
At the altar of her body's allure
Being so smitten, there is no cure.

And why would I wish to be so cured
From a condition that all would envy
Let her always rest assured
That I am hers through all eternity
Oh, may I always be so blessed
To be hers and by love caressed.

Impulses

Some of the best gratification comes
In subliminal ways
Things that tweak our libido
Unnoticed as it plays
With our subconscious
Causing us to stray
Into paths we did not expect
In our normal day to day.

The dimpled cheek, the flashing eye
The exposed neck and cleavage thus
Provokes a stimulus that makes us try
To follow the urges so aroused
Forget all else lest she passes by
And then the moment's gone
Quickly passing on the fly.

Most times it is a passing thing
A fleeting rush and then it's gone
But if followed it could bring
A meeting of two souls entwined
Making the spirit soar and sing
Love songs at heaven's gate
Not just a momentary fling.

Anniversaries

Forty-eight years have come and gone and here we sit together
Battered and bruised by all of time's hard knocks
We have stayed the course through calm and stormy weather
And the relentless ticking of the clock
As our day fades into the evening's glow
So even more does our attachment grow

Joy to the World

Today again, the news is all bad
Government mismanagement, terrorism flairs
Corruption and conflict, all so sad
And it seems that no one cares
We have become inured to awful news
No longer cause to blow a fuse

If only one morning as we awoke
The sun could shine and the birds sing
No disturbing stories would be bespoke
Only kindness and joyful things
Peace and quiet everywhere
No problems needing to be repaired

Realistically this will not be
Happy stories do not sell
Sex and violence, big melees
Are the stories people tell
It seems we enjoy the pain of others
Making our own problems feel less of a bother

Joseph Stalin said:

"ONE MAN'S DEATH IS A TRAGEDY, A MILLION MEN IS A STATISTIC"

CHAPTER TWO

Time in a Nutshell

Time in a Nutshell

As the light is fading and my breath is a dying gasp
I am trying to put into verse, before I breathe my last
Exactly how it feels to me to be at the edge of eternity
With no more tomorrows, just someone's memory.

Looking backwards on my life is like snapshots out of time
Memories of my youth when I was in my prime
My first day at school and the fear of strange new things
Learning, and the thrill that all the newness brings.

The sadness of a rejection by your first good friend
The flush of puppy love and how crushing when it ends
The bruises and the scratches earned in your first fight
The relief when it's over and everything's alright.

Moving to Canada at the age of ten
The strangeness and the loneliness of not fitting in
High School and the need to be accepted by your peers
Hiding perceived inadequacies, phobias and fears.

Quitting school at sixteen and getting my first job and pay
Trying to be an adult, and working every day
Enlisting in the Navy when the Cuban Missile Crisis dawned
Surviving Basic Training, civilian values gone

Off to Halifax and my first ship, the "Big Bold B"*
A small fish in a big pond getting by, but barely
Doing stupid adolescent stunts, lucky to not get caught
Travelling to foreign ports and the wonder that they wrought.

Drafted to my second ship, the "Sally Rand"*
A destroyer and much smaller ship,
now a more experienced hand
More foreign ports and as the time flew quickly by
My term was up and so I gave civvy streets a try.

Working in a factory was not what I desired
So I next decided to try fighting fires
I rode the rigs in Hamilton for over forty years
Through all the blood, the mud, the suffering and tears.

At the tender age twenty-three I met a special girl
We dated and then married and that changed my world
A year into our marriage, along came our first boy
A learning experience that filled our life with joy

Two years later another boy appeared upon the scene
A brother for our first son who accepted him with glee
Life in the family moved so swiftly by
Until disaster struck, my wife paralyzed for life.

Adjusting to the new ways of doing things
The struggles and the joys of all day to day things
Waking up one morning and discovering you're old
Wondering where the time went, now worth more than gold.

Wondering if I had the chance, would I do it all again
What would I do differently and what keep the same
The wonder and the mystery of the road not run
'Tis but a wistful folly, pointless now it's done.

I am truly grateful for the good things in my life
Comfort, home, family, not to mention a good wife
She has suffered much adversity, yet still is by my side
No matter how insufferable I sometimes made the ride

Now as the sands run out and time has become precious
I find a certain urgency has filled my life capricious
I am trying to get done all the things I want to do
Before it all goes black with the final turning of the screw

*"Sally Rand" H.M.C.S. St.Laurent D205.
"Big Bold B" H.M.C.S. Bonaventure C22

The Good Fight

Here alone I stand
With my hammer in my hand
Looking down that long and lonesome road
Wondering where it leads
And the curiosity it feeds
The urges to go forward that it goads.

Girded for the fight
To protect the right
Striking down the evils in your face
Moving ever forward
With no thought toward
What is coming up in the next space.

Strive forever on
When all hope is gone
Trying to stem the relentless tide
Just let "Honour Bright"
Be your beacon in the night
History and truth are on your side.

The truth does not always out
So be prepared to receive the clout
Of the doubters and the naysayers that come at you
Trust in yourself alone
At the lifting of the stone
The prize is in the right of what you do.

Joey and Macy

There were two students of McMaster Nursing School
Whose performance was away above the norm
They are warm and kind and friendly
and go well beyond the rule
Of doing what's required of them in their daily form.

They are upbeat and outgoing in their interactions
With the people in their day to day
They are co-operative and helpful in all of their transactions
And are praised by everyone along the way.

I hope that in your life you are fortunate enough
To encounter someone as praiseworthy as this pair
They make everyone around them better with their presence
And the day a little brighter from their care.

I know that when they move forward in their lives
That success will surely shower them with favour
No one as good as this pair with all they have to give
Can ever fail to prosper in their endeavours.

Futurism

The clock drips down the wall like melted wax
The floor like quicksand shifts beneath the feet
The mind shifts and distorts the facts
The noise of chaos ringing in the streets
Behold, the king has come, so let us bow
Before the symbol of almighty power
No one cares about what happens now
At the arrival of the man of the hour
Neon shines and glitz now holds sway
You cannot hear the truth above the roar
Razzle dazzle is the order of the day
Reason hangs its head, slinking out the door
As moral lines start to blur and bend
Lies and deceit seem now to be the way
The new reality has made values bend
Right and wrong is spelled differently today

Take heart, this too shall as all else, slip into the past
All is transitory, nothing ever lasts.

Acceptance

When first you meet
All is so sweet
Foibles are cute and funny,
But as time moves on
And the fun is gone
Bad habits take the sweet from the honey.

For love to succeed
You each really need
To accept each other's weird traits
When irritations arise
See them through love's eyes
And don't let anger gain weight.

The biggest mistake
That we all make
Is seeking to change the other
When all logic says
Once they're set in their ways
It's pointless to go to the bother.

Accepting them as they are
Is much better by far
Than trying to remake the wheel
Remembering the good
In your partner should
Soften the anger you feel.

Success depends on the way
That you handle each day
Which emotion you choose to shine through
Allowing love to the fore
Will soon open the door
And the irritations will vanish from you.

Lao Tzu said:

"MARRIAGE IS THREE PARTS LOVE AND SEVEN PARTS FORGIVENESS"

Aquatic Addiction

There is something very hypnotic about the sea
It draws you ever on toward its shores
On calm days the wavelets caress the beach
Like a lover's fingers that seem to promise more

In stormy weather it is unbridled power
Pounding the coast with an awesome might
Endlessly eroding the rocks hour by hour
Shaping the shoreline with its constant bite

In a craft upon its surface
The gentle rocking of the waves
Is a calming motion like a service
Designed to remove the ills of the day

There is nothing to match the unstoppable fury
Of a storm when on a ship at sea
The incredible wonder and the glory
Nature dwarfing the efforts of humanity

Once bitten by the enchanting sea
It will haunt you ever more
Drawing you constantly to be
Never far away from the ocean's roar

Your Legacy

The sands of time drift quickly by
Seemingly in the twinkling of an eye
Before you learn what you need to know
It's almost time for you to go
"Too soon old and too late smart"
Has been true right from the start
So worry not about what you've missed
But go forward in hope, life is a gift
To be used wisely day to day
Savouring what happens along the way
It's not where you are at the end of the game
But how you got there that makes your name

You Reap What You Sow

A warm summer morning and as the sun graces
A feeling of mild exhilaration greets the day
Looking forward to the tasks ahead and the friendly faces
Of the people that we know who will help along the way

If you greet the day with hope and a smile
You will usually receive the same in kind
A scowl and a curse will make life's longest mile
The one you are facing and cloud your mind

Go forth with a smile and courtesy to all you meet
And you will find that it will be returned to you
What goes around, comes around as you traverse life's streets
And the good that comes from kindness will see you through

Unwanted Changes

Often in our lives a happy situation changes
And a certain sadness then ensues
But the one true constant that time arranges
Is that everything soon passes from our view

We cannot stop the changes or time's ceaseless beat
So absorb the change and move on
Be glad you had it for a moment and greet
The new situation now the old one is gone.

Most times this is easier said than done
But we must adjust to it and move on

Tropical Time Frame

The sun turns the pavement to liquid tar
There's no relief from the blazing sun
Music drifts through the open doors of a bar
Movement is kept to what has to be done.

The heat of the day is not the time
To be moving or working out of doors
Down here in the tropical climes
It's do what you must and then no more.

Those from more temperate zones don't get
The way time moves to a different beat
No sense of urgency, no need to sweat
It'll all get done in a time that's meet.

There's a lesson to be learned for the willing few
There's no need to panic about the day to day
"Don't sweat the small shit" just pay what's due
And the rest will follow along in its own way.

To Serve and Protect

With all the strength left in my arm
I will defend her to the very last
Guard and protect her from all harm
Keep her safe and happy, as in the past
Her happiness is all the reward I need
The manna on which my soul shall feed.

'Tis the Season

As the winter solstice nears and the Yuletide comes again
All is laughter and "bonhomie", generosity holds sway
Yet, still the world is full of suffering, want and pain
If only all of that could stop, even for a single day

Would that not truly be the spirit of "good cheer"
The milk of human kindness spread both far and near
The homeless warm and safe and free from fear
The almost perfect ending to another disastrous year

If each of us would do even one single kindly deed
Brightening up some unfortunate's hard, unforgiving lot
To ease for just a moment their endless want and need
Costing you very little considering the superfluity you've got

So next time you see a beggar cadging his way along
Don't think of them as an annoyance and move quickly on
Give them a smile and any gift you can afford
The warmth you'll feel inside you will be your best reward

Then, don't let the sentiment die once the seasons past
Carry it in your heart the whole year over
Don't let this brief moment of kindness be your last
And you'll find that happiness will be yours forever

Through the Tough Times

There are times in your life when things go sour
All seems bad and the troubles look insurmountable
This is where you have to live hour to hour
And keep swimming against the tide that appears unstoppable
You only fail if you stop trying
This too shall pass so stop crying

Get on with the road that lies ahead
Nothing stays the same, everything's changing
It only ends when you are dead
Keep your chin up start rearranging
Things will get better on the morrow
Dry your tears and end the sorrow

Come the morn, the sun will shine
The clouds will clear, the sun break through
You will survive and things will be fine
Simply keep trying and you'll find that you
Will come through the other side alive
Brighter times will come and you will thrive

The Tides of Life

The rolling tides
The dolphins play
The ships move by
Along their way
The horizon calls
Ever on
Here for now
Tomorrow gone
Restless, moving
Ever changing
Always proving
Time is rearranging
All is transitory
Nothing lasts
Life is fleeting
Oh, so fast
Enjoy today
To soon it's gone
Time moves forever on.

The Panoply of Life

As my age advances I find that I
Am still amazed at the kaleidoscope of life
People never cease to amaze and delight the eye
The variety of shapes, and actions that are rife.

The young, the old, and in between, in an endless parade
The wise, the weird, the coward, the brave,
The curious, the indifferent, how we are all made
The cruel, the kind and how they behave.

To sit on a bench in the city's centre and study
The restless moving stream of humanity
The polite, the rude, the bully, the fuddy-duddy
The beggar, the addict, the peacock's vanity.

What is the story behind them all
What made them turn out this way
What subtle nudge lead their feet to fall
On the path they tread today.

Unanswered questions to untold stories
Whether a prince or pauper be
All a part of the greater glory
Of the wonder of humanity.

Thoughts of Love

When she's not there time seems to stand still
When she's not there the day drags slowly by
When she's not there then gone is the thrill
Of accomplishing the things I try
But when she returns so does the shining sun
And the light of pleasure has begun.

Time spent apart is not an evil thing
Since familiarity tends to breed contempt
Each day spent elsewhere only brings
A more heightened pleasure for the time that's spent
Together in a warm and loving place
Culminating in the tenderest embrace.

So as our daily life spreads us apart
The thought of the coming evening tends to bring
A happy glow of warmth into the heart
That lightens up the day and makes the soul sing
For the time together that we spend
Is time that I wish would never end.

The "Or Else" Factor

The only thing controlling one's actions in their life
Is the thought of the retribution to follow
Cause and effect and the resulting strife
Is what will control all of your tomorrows

Punishment and reward is religion's foundation
Your actions, good or bad, decide your fate
Whether an eternity in hell as a retribution
Or elysian fields of happiness through heaven's gate

Doing what is right gives one a sense of pride
A feeling that is its own reward
Malfeasance leaves one with a darker side
Bad feelings that are hard to disregard

To me the best things are the ones
That no one knows about, you don't leave a trace
Of the kind deed that when it's done
Makes someone else's life a better place

Goodness is it's own reward and feeds upon itself
It leads to more good deeds and personal pleasure
Bad things, even though they may lead to power and pelf
Will fade away and provide no lasting pleasure

The Not So Shiny Prize

How often in life do we wish for a thing
To be disappointed at the lack of pleasure it brings
When we finally achieve that craved for prize
It's not all that we thought as we strived
To arrive at the object of our desire
Dry ashes in the mouth, not the moment of fire.

When you finally get what you were craving for
It sometimes leaves you thinking that there must be more
Disappointment will leave you feeling flat
Realizing that this was not where it's at
Too many times it's not what we hoped it to be
Is simply just a fact of reality.

So heed the lesson and take some advice
Before you wish, be sure to think twice
That the yearned for thing you were focused on
Will only shine 'til it's in your palm
The glow will fade and desire will find
The bright new treasure next in line.

The Kiss of Elpis

When you are in that black despair and you want to pull the pin
And there seems to be no way out of the place you're in
Remember there are no "do overs", you only get one shot
So try to make the best of it no matter what you've got

A kind and loving arm around your shoulders would be nice
A "chin up mate" from someone close could really break the ice
But when you're out there by yourself and all alone
Yours is the only voice you'll hear to guide you safely home

Rely upon yourself, you see, must be your guiding light
And if you hark unto it, it will get you through the night
Into the dawn of a new tomorrow when the sun will beam
And hope that springs eternal shall complete your dream

The Religion of Love

The one true God is Eros and when he whispers in your ear
It is almost impossible to resist the seeds he spreads
You will drive ever forward, conquering any fear
To gain the object of your love, regardless of the dread.

Once gained and it is returned in kind
Paradise is within each other's grasp
The tender kisses, touches and embrace
All leads to two hearts enclasped.

The passion of two hearts desire
Strikes a flame much stronger
Than any a church could inspire
And it will last much longer.

To worship at the altar of each other's love
Is to achieve the perfect heaven
It is a rare and precious gift from above
So take it not lightly when it's given.

Nurture and tend it like a priceless flower
Basking in the bliss of every heaven-sent hour.

Oceanus

The sea is a fascinating timeless thing
Restless and changing, never still
At times serene, then a storm will bring
A fury and power that can kill.

All through time man has tried
To harness the bounty of the great waters
Predicting the weather and the tides
For catching food, or the battle's slaughter.

Children play in the tidal pools
Or build large castles in the sand
Lovers stroll hand in hand in the jewels
At the water's edge where the waves lap the land.

It's still the best way to transport wares
Hither and yon, throughout the Earth
Technology is such that it reduces the cares
Of the route and the dangers of any worth.

Yet still the caprice of Nature's way
Can make sea travel a risky thing
The rise of a sudden storm will play
Havoc on schedules and the delays it brings.

From mild to majestic to fearsome thing
Amusement to children, a living for some
Powerful or gentle, each mood brings
Changes and chances to all who come.

Dark of the Moon

Night descends and quiet creeps in
The unknown things that dwell in the dark
Bats flit by on silent wings
In the distance a coyote barks.

In the oak tree an owl hoots warning
Footsteps echo in the empty way
The world slumbers on in wait of morning
A cat slinks by in search of prey.

The daytime denizens rest and sleep
The night prowlers continuous move around
Each has it's place in the ordered creep
Of time as it moves ever onward bound.

The dark is not evil, it just hides these things
Since the human eye is designed for light
Primordial fears let the imagination bring
On irrational fears of the night.

Demons and goblins and witches spring bold
Images of beasts running rampant and wild
Stories take on a reality when told
Imbedded deep in the mind of a child.

Hence, as adults we have a built-in switch
And thusly when the darkness falls
Every little sound makes us start and twitch
At the thought of the creatures beyond our walls.

Worry yourself not about unseen things
Believe in the reality you can see and feel
Everything else is but imaginings
Of demons in the mind that are not real.

So it is with the problems we traverse
Each day in our journey, ever on
The anticipation of trouble is usually worse
Than the reality of it once it's gone!

Changing of the Guard

And so begins a new era in our Civic Cemeteries
The old superintendent left for greener fields
We now have a "temporary" person for the in between
The "old" and "new" and what the future will yield

As usual, there were mixed feelings about the old
Those that liked, those that didn't, the
trouble that they wrought
But when it comes right down to it if the truth be told
The "old" was really not as bad as they thought

The new one may not be worse or be better
But, they will be different that's for sure
The new broom that sweeps clean, a real go-getter
Will ruffle feathers as they seek to score

Only time will tell what the truth will be
A year from now after the settling of the dust
Once all the foofar wanes you will see
That nothing really changed for all the fuss

The ones that liked the old will adjust or quit
The ones that hated will be temporarily glad
Until they find that the new is not so great a fit
And they're no better off than what they had

The rising stars will rise no matter what
The dead wood will quietly fall away
People will learn to work with what they've got
The sun will rise and shine on another day

The Loving Cup

She is the cup from which I drink
To slake my unquenchable loving thirst
My love for her is so deep I think
That sometimes my poor heart will burst.
Ah, my dream will be complete
If I can make her soul replete.

Starts the Day

In the early morning, as I begin to wake
And the sight of my love sleeping fills my eyes
I bless the day I found her, and the way she makes
My soul soar to great heights and fills my life
With a joy I cannot ever fully express
Being with her makes my life a success.

If I can but make her wishes all come true
Then I will feel that I have served my role
Fulfilling the destiny that I was born to do
Giving her my heart, my soul, my all
My life's ambition will truly be replete
And my Nirvana will be so complete.

Letting Go

One of the hardest things to do is admitting when you're wrong
Backing off from a position that you hold dear
Accepting that you must rethink, lest before so very long
Things will get so much worse than they are here.

There comes a time when you must cut your losses and admit
That no matter what you do you cannot win
The point that you were making simply does not fit
Into the situation that you are now in.

Often you have so much money and time
Invested in the current event
You think you cannot afford to decline
Having sunk too much into it to relent

Cut your losses and save time and exertion
Throw not good money after bad
Accept that this is a losing proposition
Resign yourself to it and be not sad.

A gambler's downfall comes when he's in so deep
That he thinks his only out is to chase
The rabbit down the hole and so he keeps
Doubling down, hoping to recoup his grace.

Fight only the battles that you feel you must
Waste not your time and effort in losing causes
Move on towards more hopeful thrusts
Cast off the ones that are filled with flaws.

Summer's Bliss

A warm summer morning and a haze hugs the ground
A gentle breeze is blowing, the air is sweeter and fresher
Life is great and wonderful with hope all around
All it needs is someone with whom to share the pleasure

With the one you love beside you the moment's even better
Here is Nirvana, completed with a kiss
All else falls away, the senses heighten to the letter
Nothing can come close to this moment's bliss

All too soon the world intrudes and the spell is broken
But the aura of this time still lingers yet
Two hearts entwined together with no word spoken
Lifts the soul of each to the other so well met

Elysian Fields

Not a day goes by that I do not bless
My good fortune to live in so happy a place
Far from the troubles, the turmoil and the mess
Of other countries that are lacking our grace

We live in an idyllic land so rife
With forests, lakes, mountains and rivers
Teeming with every kind of wild life
Natural pleasures that will make you shiver

Opportunity abounds at every turn
A good life is there for the taking
With determination you can earn
Your desires, all for the making

Ontario can fulfill your every need
To be made from the sweat of your brow
Nothing is free so go plant the seed
The path to your future is now

Elpis Versus Moros

When you awaken in the morning and wanes the fog of sleep
You will find yourself thinking on the problems of the day
Remembering that crisis that you're into very deep
Once solved, only leads to the next one on the way
For life is merely problem solving as you try to clasp
The gold ring which lies just beyond your grasp

So heed unto Elpis who will whisper in your ear
That if you just do this you will finally reach
That all elusive Nirvana which appears so very near
Believing in a goal that experience should teach
Is really not quite achievable in life
For life is but a treadmill of ceaseless strife

If you listen unto Moros it will only lead to fright
To depression and a tendency to leave
Believing in the impossible will give you the might
To swim against the tide and to achieve
That which you thought could never be done
And so bask in the victory that you have won

Believing in the impossible will make you ever stronger
Fight the good fight regardless, forever onward
Toward that pot of gold which will elude you no longer
For Victory in itself is it's own reward
Bring on the next problem you can greet
It and forever stave off defeat

Civic Insanity

The Civic Management leaders in their infinite wisdom decreed
That the culture of the work force needed to be changed
So they hired a consulting firm to determine what was needed
And told the employees that things would be rearranged
They even called in some of the workers
to exchange some thoughts
Hoping to bring about the wonders to be wrought

When all was said and done they then turned around
And did not solve the problems that the consultant had found
Instead upper management left things as they had been
Confounding middle management who were trapped in between
And thus things continued on as they always were
Nothing changed, it was the" same old", no demur

Albert Einstein said

"INSANITY IS DOING THE SAME THING OVER AND OVER AGAIN AND EXPECTING A DIFFERENT RESULT"

Souls Entwined

In the woods hand in hand with no words bespoke
Revelling in the closeness with satiating pleasure
Only by the twittering birds is the silence broke
The union of two souls radiates love without measure.
Hearts entwined like fingers gripping one another
Ah, 'tis paradise here on earth between two lovers.

Ease the Moment

When all is in a blather
And you would really rather
Be anywhere else on this particular day
Just briefly close your eyes
And think on clear blue skies
And let the turmoil simply slip away.

Things will not disappear
Because you let your mind clear
But it will help to put things in perspective
Then you can collect
Your thoughts and select
That which is most important and needs directives.

Take a deep breath and sigh
And open up your eyes
And you will find things take a slower pace
Then buckle up and start
To play your active part
And the confusion will all sort out into its place.

Joy in Life

The human mind has many moods
That swing wildly to and fro
Love and hate, happy and sad
Following the happenstance as it goes
Back and forth in our daily life
Through success and failure as both are rife.

The most powerful of all is love of course
It gives the most satisfaction and peace
Building, productive with gentle force
It shapes our lives with grace and ease
To receive it is joy in contented streams
To give it is pleasure beyond your dreams.

Anger and hatred are corrosive and defeating
Eroding the soul in all that they touch
Becoming a habit that is oft repeating
Withering the person's life so much
Let old quarrels and wrongs fade into the past
Let warmth and love be the things that last.

The love of a kindred spirit and friends
Will make your world a happy place
When an effort collapses at it's end
Comfort from loved ones is the solace
The tie that binds and eases the pain
So that you can regroup and try again.
Carrying a grudge is an onerous load
It bends the back and corrodes the soul
It sets your feet on a thankless road
That in the end will swallow you whole
Slough off your anger and you will find
The kindness of love will fill your mind.

Insomnia

Three in the morning and sleep won't come
Tossing and turning, the harder you try
The further your rest seems to slip from
Your grasp and disappear on the fly.

The mind wanders aimlessly through time
A kaleidoscope of snapshots of things past
The good seeming to be sublime
The bad, much worse, time moves so fast

Wondering where old friends are today
Did they succeed, do they still live
What would have been if I'd gone that way
What does the future have to give

Plans and things that did not occur
Surprising outcomes unexpected
Futures planned that got blurred
By events not suspected

Life is a journey, enjoy the ride
Don't fret over things gone by
Time moves on, go with the tide
Tomorrow's coming on the fly

She is My Gift

She is the moon in my sky
The sun on a day that's fine
I will always endeavour to try
To make her life as happy as she makes mine
That fortune has given me her to love
Is truly a gift from heaven above.

Finality

I sat and held your hand as you slipped quietly away
Your hand went limp as you breathed your last
Your eyes went empty and there's nothing more to say
Your presence now has slipped into the past.

The happiness and joy you spread will live forever on
Beside the empty sadness and the hollow that you left
The lives you touched will continue even though you are gone
But your absence will leave everyone bereft.

A part of being human is that sooner or later we all die
And those we leave behind will mourn our departure
But the legacy we leave behind should help to dry
The tears of our loved ones as they move into the future.

Take heart in the fact that the inevitable end
Of life is death and it awaits us all
Let the good we do add to the mosaic of life's blend
Outweighing the bad in us as we answer the final call.

Imaginings

Man's spirit soars on imagination's wings
Thoughts on cat's paws creep in to plant the seed
Ambition then drives one to do great things
Thus the thought is father to the deed

If not for that impossible dream
Man would never have taken flight
Newton's apple evoked a lump and a scheme
That brought today's physics into the light

Great deeds, great works and great art
Spring from the brain fired by the heart
Without emotions stoking the fire
None of these things would have transpired

Without strong feelings the imagination
Would not be able to reach for the stars
But instead would languish in stagnation
Never growing or reaching out so far

Happenstance

The sun rises upward
The night recedes
The road stretches forward
The journey proceeds
Life slides by
On swift silent feet
Old age is nigh
Youth retreats
The promise of tomorrow
That never arrives
The pain and the sorrow
Overcome and survived
The moment's pleasure
Of a blessed thing
Things you can treasure
Make the heart sing
Struggle and strife
Well meaning intent
All this is life
So just be content
As onward you strive
Be glad you're alive!

Defeating Consternation

When the hounds of hell are nipping at your heels
And you are all alone, at least that's how you feel
Lean on another's shoulder, take a breath and rest
A pause is all you need to be fully at your best.

You'll gather strength from someone else's kindness
Just realize that the blather is all mindless
Caused by cretins, not worth your spent emotion
They try to gain strength from causing the commotion.

Calm your Wa and set your thoughts in an array
Head held high and onward into the fray
Your honest efforts will yet win out the day
A grand example that will show the way.

Good Deeds

Doing something nice for someone else is so rewarding
To yourself and the recipient of the deed
It gives to both a sense of warmth and kindness regarding
The human condition that is in desperate need
Of all the gentleness it can gather
From interaction with each other.

As the world becomes more crowded day by day
It is imperative that we learn to be
More considerate of our neighbour's ways
And how we behave interactually
"Do as you would be done by" should be the rule
Peace and harmony our shining jewel.

Reunited

When I am awaiting for my love to arrive
The anticipation builds up as I wait
My senses are honed like the edge of a knife
And the expectation makes my heart palpitate
The culmination that the arrival brings
Is truly a satisfyingly wondrous thing.

The first embrace and tender greeting kiss
Erases all the sorrow of the absence
The pleasure of her closeness is such bliss
That time stands still in the aura of her presence
She is my world and all that I could wish
Nirvana pales in comparison to this.

Quiet Moments

I walked beside my love with our hands entwined
In the summer gloaming at the closing of the day
Two hearts and minds as one with all troubles left behind
Silent in the moment, with our hearts at play
A love so completely sublime as this
Can only lead to a culminating kiss

Her touch, her warmth and her serenity
Defy my ability to voice my love
Would that I had the verbal dexterity
To entirely express my feelings and to prove
That she is the centre of my universe
And that there is nothing that I would reverse

Geriatrocity

Once more I have presented myself at the geriatric place
To be poked and prodded, handled and appeased
By people who are more interested in research than my face
I'm just another stat in the data bank if you please.

Old people don't matter, they're just taking up space
And resources that could be used in a better plan
On young people who have a more important place
In the grand scheme of things, than a worn out old man.

And so I play my part and meekly nod and agree
To all that they suggest I do and get bored
Then when it is over carry on and I am free
Turned loose to take up space and be ignored.

I really do not like feeling like a useless lump
I would like to think that my remaining time
Could be spent as something other than a chump
Such as sitting spinning out my rhymes.

Perhaps my tinkering could help others understand
That old people are still people, regardless of their age
They need to feel useful and treated well, not out of hand
Remember, they were once young and
strong, holding centre stage.

Futile Hopes

I never cease to be amazed
At the regularity of empty pleas
For help from a God who seems unfazed
By the mayhem and suffering that he sees
When trouble strikes most people pray
"Oh God, please help me through this day."

If the Good Lord did not see fit to prevent
The trouble happening, then why would you
Expect that he will help you now the event
Has occurred, correcting things to see you through
To happier times when this has eased
Because you prayed on bended knees.

Look not to heaven or to the skies
For help from this indifferent being
Rely upon yourself and strive
Against the problem you are seeing
The answer lies within your heart
Not in some dogmatic religious part.

From the Back Seat

Riding through the night in the back seat of a car
Gazing from the window at the snippets in the dark
The lights of a farm house signalling life from afar
The humming of the tires on the blacktop so stark
The miles slip endless by as the clock ticks ceaselessly
The mind tends to wander and thoughts come randomly

Wondering at the tales you are passing on the road
The stars that shine above you, eternal in the sky
Who else is staring at them and the future that they bode
Who are we and what's the meaning of it all and why
Are we all here swimming in this great sea of life
Constantly wrestling with the happiness and strife

Is it all a grand plan, or perhaps just random chance
Is it all predestined, or are we the masters of our fate
Are we just puppets being led through an infernal dance
Is there a benevolent being awaiting at the gate
As we pass through into what lies beyond the pale
Or is it just an empty void hidden behind the veil

At last the journey ends and your thoughts turn to today
All the rest forgotten drifts quietly away

Mall Watching

Sitting in the Glendale Galleria Mall
Watching as the world goes by
It strikes me that no matter whether large or small
Or where ever in the world you try
The scenery is exactly the same
It seems the only change is the store names.

There's young and old in varying shades
There's shoppers and walkers and watchers
There's people as sharp as the edge of a blade
And others who are truly sight catchers
The rushed, the harried, the fast, the slow
All a part of the kaleidoscope on show.

The doddering old who are going no place
Spending their days amid the swirl
The young couples with love in their face
Sales people with a line to unfurl
All drawn to this place of commerce and trade
Some aimless, some full of plans to be made.

It is truly a microcosm of life at large
With all aspects covered in full strength
Entertainment before you at no charge
There to be viewed and pondered at length
Wondering at the untold stories
The drama before you in all it's glories.

Life at Sea

The wind hurls the spray from the wave crown
And it stings the eyes and face
The falling bow of the ship plunging down
Beyond the crest into the empty space
Left as the wave rolls under the keel
The quartermaster fighting the unruly wheel.

As the ship struggles on through the storms rage
Heeling, heaving and bucking along
The men of the crew work through this stage
Of the trip as though nothing is wrong
Just another occasion of nautical strife,
It's merely a blip on the graph of life.

Down below in the engineering spaces
The engine room gang go through their paces
Of tweaking, adjusting and checking gauges
Impervious to all of the weather's rages
The bilge water sloshes beneath the deck plates
The occasional word passed between their mates.

In the mess decks the off-watch crew at ease
Sitting reading, talking, or in their bunks asleep
Time to relax and do as you please
'Til it's time to return to the duty you keep
Whether up above or down below
Maintaining the ships progress on the go.
Each crew member is an integral part
Of the team that is the ship's company
Everyone performing from the start
Duties that mesh in planned harmony
A group effort that make the ship a living soul,
Moving ever onward toward their goal

Arriving in port and storm's damage shows plain
And obvious for the ship's bosun to see
Getting the deck gang to work on the main
Of the peeled off paint and the rust streaks
Readying the ship for the next journey they plumb
No matter the caprices of nature to come.

K'ung Fu Tzu

Confucius was the Latinised name
K'ung Fu Tzu in his native tongue
A Chinese philosopher of lasting fame
Was a government official when still quite young
His teachings are wise and still apply today
He is credited with authoring the "Golden Rule"
Which all children should accept as the one true way
Before their very first day at school.

"Do not do to others that which you
Do not want done to yourself" is proof
Of the wisdom of the master K'ung Fu Tzu
The first of his teachings of the great truths
Of life and the way to conduct yourself
In dealing with others in the day to day
Not just the mindless grasp for pelf
In life's journey along the way.

The end result which awaits us all
Is the cemetery and the final end
Whether we have been great or small
All deeds fade away as we descend
Unto the dust from whence we sprung
And our only lasting imprint will be
How we performed as our life's song was sung
And what we left for posterity.

K'ung Fu Tzu clearly saw that the way
Of goodness and kindness and respect
Of those around us and those of olden days
Will bring order from chaos and deflect
The evils of selfishness from our lives
Softening cruelty and spreading humanity
So that everyone can derive
A decent life and equanimity.

He truly showed that the destination
Is not as important as the route
That we travel through life's molestations
Shouldering gently each dispute
Treating each other with respect and gentility
Will soften the blows that come our way
Dispelling anger and revenge which are a futility
Sowing seeds of good for a future day.

Instead of religious prejudices and hate
We all should learn from K'ung Fu Tzu
That respect and tolerance opens more gates
Than violence and bigotry will ever do
The other man's ideas are as good as yours
Respect his thoughts on an equal plain
You cannot change his social mores
With force or laws or military gains.

Good deeds come back in kind
Accept that which you cannot change
Someone else's thoughts in their mind
Will not by force be rearranged
Beliefs which spring up from the heart
Can only be changed through willingness
Kindness and respect will from the start
Lead to understanding and progress.

Good things outlast the teacher's lives
Hence K'ung Fu Tzu's teachings show
That goodness lasts and truths survive
As evils pass away and go
Into the pages of the past
And truth and beauty will shine through
Honour and respect will stand fast
Because they are eternal truths.

Order and Symmetry

The Universe is founded on symmetry and order
All things in their place interacting well
When something's out of sync it brings on disorder
And chaos and confusion start to swell.

When one part of the equation is dysfunctionally aligned
It disrupts the entire symmetry and fusion
Throwing out of order the parts that are conjoined
And thus the whole system's cohesion.

Hence when one person does harm to another,
Whether it was planned or untoward
Focus not on revenge and all it's bother
But just repair the damage and move ever forward.

You cannot change what's happened or undo the deed
The bell once struck cannot be unrung
But you can move forward to fulfill the need
Brought on by what the misstep had begun.

Revenge is nothing but an empty glass
It promises much but gives absolutely nil
It absorbs time and effort that could be amassed
In helping other aims to be fulfilled.

Nirvana

Nirvana, distant shimmers in the noonday sun
At the end of the rainbow where tomorrow never comes
The unquenchable thirst for the things you do not have
That everyone is chasing just as fast as they can

With Mastercard and Visa, Platinum and Gold
You can reach Nirvana, at least that's what we're told
It's only just around the corner, a little further down
We will be showered with fame, fortune and renown

What they are not telling you is of the hidden cost
The price you pay in money and time all gets lost
On the endless treadmill trying to reach that field of dreams
Hovering on the horizon in the patchwork of your dreams

Madison Avenue convinces you that you need that push up bra
Power windows and heated seats in your expensive car
To bring that bit of heaven into your life today
It really doesn't cost too much (until you come to pay)

You must remember "Carpe Diem", seize the day
Life is what happens to you as you plan the way
You reach your own Elysian Fields, so elusive in the mist
Not missing out on the moment that you are holding in your fist

CHAPTER THREE

Sands of Time

The Sands of Time

Time is a river flowing ever on
Unstoppable as it wends it's way to the sea
A leaf upon it's surface is so very quickly gone
Into the distant past of you and me
One never knows when your turn will be contrived
But, rest assured, it is looming and it will arrive.

Live in the moment so that you do not miss
All the wonder that your time can deliver
Pleasure and pain's passing is so swift
It comes and goes as quickly as a shiver
Enjoy each happening as it will not remain
Once gone it will come no more again.

Precious Moments

The night creeps in and covers the world
The bustle of the day fades slowly out
Troubles wane as peace unfurls
A gentle breeze moves the leaves about.

The hiss of the wavelets kissing the shore
Hand in hand on an empty beach
Who could possibly ask for more
Romance rules to the end of the senses reach.

Tomorrow the din of the world will abound
But for now just savour the moments bliss
Speechless, Nirvana has now been found
Capped off with a stolen kiss

The Barrier of Age

Time creeps past on cat's paws unnoticed and unheeded
The future stretches out in endless days you deem
'Til one morning you notice that more time has preceded
Than what you have ahead and where are all your dreams.

You start to scratch off your list all the trivial things
That do not count for much in the overall grand flight
Of your life and the legacy you'll leave when death brings
Down the curtain and you slip into the eternal night.

Be not disheartened in the thought that the end is near
Just be more determined to complete things that really matter
Spend your time on people and things
that you hold so very dear
Enjoy each bite of the feast of life that's left on your platter.

Passion's Moment

The merest touch of the finger exciting the skin
The brush of the lips on the curve of the neck
The catch of the breath signals arousal within
All points to the start of a passion unchecked
Arms now entwined with bodies as one
Bring forth the crescendo, leaving neither undone.

As the moment subsides and the float back to earth
The warmth of affection fills the empty space
That the passion now expended leaving a dearth
Which is filled with the love on each other's face.
The nearness, the love, the glow of two hearts
Forever together, never to part.

My Life

She fills my life with love and peace
Stability and comfort, warmth and pleasure
A firm grounding and a life of ease
Memories and hope of moments to treasure
She is my life and all I need
The sustenance on which my heart doth feed.

Surviving the Storm

The bow crests the wave and then careens
Into the trough and buries itself deep
The fo'c'sle awash in the dark gray-green
Of the ocean's vast and endless creep
The stern rising up, the props swinging free
'Til gravity forces it back into the sea

Wave after wave, in seeming endless lines
The storm-tossed water heaving ceaselessly
Wind whipped spume off the crests stings the eyes
The pounding a relentless cacophony
The beauty and fury of a storm at sea
Is always an awesome thing to me

But after the storm comes rest and calm
The sun shines brightly, the sea birds perform
The sea turns blue, the waves a rolling balm
Following the powerful anger of the storm
So it is with things in life
All things pass, even the strife

Summer's Heat

Six in the morning and the thermometer stands
At twenty-four degrees Celcius in the shade
Heat waves are shimmering off the land
And plants are slowly wilting more each day
The sun beats down with a merciless heat
The pavement bubbles beneath your feet.

People constantly complain about the heat
Sweating and moaning without relent
Just remember when February's frigid beat
Was freezing all with vicious intent
Enjoy what you have before it passes by
Leaving only fond memories in the mind's eye.

The mind always casts back to times in the past
And remembers them with a fondness not felt at the time
Bad things are remembered as worse, more aghast
Good times are exaggerated and thought more sublime
Think on each day as an opportunity
And relish the moment with pleasure and glee.

Mihi Omnes

She stepped into my life and she completed me
She is all I could ever want or need
She is my all and forever will be
The manna on which my soul will feed
Without her my life would be an empty space
There is nothing on earth that could take her place

When I am sad her loving warmth enfolds me
Her tenderness causes all my pains to ease
She is the joy that lightens all life's sorrows
And in her arms, all my troubles cease
Without her my heart would cease to beat
If I could I would lay the world at her feet

Ad Finem Vitae

Before us lies the mortal coil of one who has now left,
Fled from this vale of tears and woe, unto his great reward
He was known to many and loved by some who are now bereft
And must carry on with life without
his presence and his warmth.

We shall remember him in life and how he was
Laughing, happy, somber, wise, human with all his flaws.

We should not dwell on his faults and the wrongs of the past
But neither should we sanctify him as better than he was
Rather let us tell the truth and let the good that will last
Go beyond his days and benefit those to whom he gave pause.

Let those who gained from his presence
be thankful that they met
And profit from the lessons learned and
the wisdom that they get.

Thusly let us sit in silence and remember our good friend
Neither a saint nor a sinner, just a man with feet of clay
Who lived his life to the fullest, right up to the end
Let the good live on forever and the rest just fade away.

There was more good than bad in him, when all is said and done
May he rest easy and at peace, now that his race is run.

Simple Pleasures

The wind in the willows
The sun on the pines
Wavelets kissing the beach
On a day so fine
That time should stand still
And everlastingly fill
The cup of life's bliss
Should ever be this.

Canada

On the anniversary of Canada's birth
I cast my mind on what it means to me
To be Canadian and all the worth
Of living in a land so free.

I am not a Canadian by birth
I am a Canadian by choice, you see
Of all the places on this earth
There is nowhere else I'd rather be.

Land of forests, land of lakes
Land of mountains, land replete
Land of everything it takes
To make life happily complete.

Home of chances for the taking
Opportunity beyond one's wildest dreams
Hope and success ready for the making
The answer to a dreamer's schemes.

Everything you could ever need
Laid before you for the asking
All it takes is to do the deed
And reap the rewards of your tasking.

I hear daily people groaning
Of this injustice, sad songs to sing
Instead of all the useless moaning
Do something positive to change these things.

Look at things with a positive view
Every day is a brand new slate
Canada is a gift for you
Opportunity awaits you at the gate.

On the news each day misery unfolds
Starving people, homeless refugees
Strife that makes the blood run cold
At the fate of ones not as fortunate as we.

So on this day and throughout the year
Be sure to give thanks and bless this land
Revel in the good fortune and hold dear
That which we each have in our hand

Love's Remedy

Life is oh so beautiful when love fills your heart
Problems seem to pale and everything seems better
Sensations are more heightened and the clouds will part
All is so easy and the spirit is unfettered.

Without love life is an empty place
But when it comes it fills the vacuous space.

A lover's touch will quickly soothe the pain
Smoothing the wrinkles of a worried brow
A warm embrace can always help you gain
An even keel, ah were heaven enow.

Love is the thing that stays the strife
Bringing order out of chaos in your life.

Urgent Care

Life has been called "a vale of tears"
It seems aptly to apply to the waiting room
Of this Urgent Care Centre and those waiting here
For their turn for treatment so that they can zoom
Back to their life as it was before
The malady which brought them to this door

The old, the young, the in-between
The smart, the stupid, and all the rest
A polyglot of the human scene
All lumped together as a guest
Of the Fates which brought them here
To this place of suffering and fear

Most will leave quite content
With the treatment they've received
Some will find that they'll been sent
Elsewhere to have their condition relieved
Once in a while the odd one departs
In the Funeral Directors cart

Day by day the wheel turns
The procession of pain continues unchecked
The broken thumb, the barbeque burn
The skate boarder with a gash on his neck
Sooner or later they will all cycle past
The "vale of tears" into which they've been cast

Zero I.Q.

John von Munchausen prattles endlessly on
Like a brook who's babbling is never gone
Ceaseless and mindless, cretinously
Drubbing on the minds of you and me.

If only he could see how he is wearing
Out his welcome and his mouth is tearing
A hole in his own credibility
Until nothing is left but insanity.

Robert Burns said:

"WOULD THAT GOD THE SENSE HAD GI'E US TO SEE OURSELVES AS OTHERS SEE US"

Shifting Sands

The one thing in life that is constant is change
Nothing stays the same for very long at all
Getting used to something only to have it rearranged
Can be frustrating, if it ends a good thing's thrall

Expecting anything to last is like shouting in the wind
It only makes you hoarse and your throat sore
It accomplishes nothing and is futile in the end
So enjoy it while it lasts for it will come no more

So live in the moment and be prepared to cope
With all the changes as they come around
For soon this will pass and you can only hope
That the next thing in the line is pleasing found

Summer Enchantment

A warm summer morning and a soft rain is falling
The dry earth absorbs the drops with thanks
All living things are grateful for the calling
Of the water from the clouds dark banks

The summer is a time for growth and love
Everything springs forth in gay profusion
The suns warmth is a blessing from above
Life is a full and joyous explosion

May the summer of youth and love last forever
Joy and love and laughter all mixed together

Self-Centered People

You see it every day and are probably guilty too
Of pushing your needs ahead of others around
Trying to jump the line because there's things you need to do
Impatient simply because your life is so tightly wound.

You do not stop to think of the people that you harm
By forcing your way past them in the wait
But should someone else barge past you,
you will grab them by the arm
And try to make them take their place proceeding to the gate.

You see it all the time on YouTube and the news
Fights in line-ups for tickets to a show
Road rage is an example of people with a short fuse
Proof that the ridiculous is everywhere you go.

Next time the situation arises just take a step back
Take a deep breath and let it slowly out
The five minutes you think you're saving is not worth the lack
Of manners and kindness we all need without a doubt.

If we could all just be a little nicer to each other
Instead of thinking only of number one
It would remove so much of the hassle and the bother
And make the world much nicer when we're done.

Love Refreshed

Early in the morning with the sun shining off the dew
And everything seems so clean and fresh and new
The spirits soar into the cloudless sky so blue
All is a golden promise of a day that's coming true.
With her beside me I know all will be well
The heart swells with emotions that no words can tell.

Relationships

Relationships are difficult and hard to understand
What first attracted you to each other when it all began
Was it physical or mental or an emotional draw
That brought you together and the start of it all

Whatever it was, it obviously grew
And blossomed into love as the months flew
'Til some years had passed and the bloom was off the rose
The novelty wore off and the warts start to show

Here's where it starts to get quite complicated
Idiosyncrasies that were cute now become outdated
Each feels that they're on the short end of the stick
Thus if it's not worked on by both, it can get nasty quick

Forgiveness and not carrying a grudge must ensue
In order for the love to return to you
A kind word and an apology from both will help take
The sting from the argument you both helped make

The warmth you find in each other's arms
Will soon assist in rebuilding all the charm
Returning you both to the feeling you held
Back in the beginning when your hearts started to meld

Cemetery Sights

August and the ever present heat is a constant glow
The tar on the road is a semi-liquid consistency
The hearse pulls through the gate with the cavalcade in tow
The staff stands by to fill the grave when the last ones go.

Loved ones gather 'round the grave all misty eyed
The hole a cruel cut taken from the manicured earth
Then one takes the lead and starts the process of goodbyes
Each one mourning in their own particular dearth.

No one wants to be the first to leave the site
Lingering on when there's nothing more to say
'Til finally a person takes a step to the right
And moves away from the bier though others stay.

Finally they all drift toward the road
Climbing in their vehicles and start to move
Once the last of them is gone the staff go into burial mode
Like a well oiled machine that's found it's groove.

The casket is lowered and the dressings are folded away
The truck backs in with a fresh load of earth
Once full and raked the flowers are placed and so convey
A sense of finality to the funeral's worth.

Another member has joined the vast club of those
Who have gone before to lead the way
An end to this person's life's struggles and woes
To rest in peace, at least that's what we pray.

Ponderings

While sitting on my own in meditation
I start to think on some introspective things
On life and love and my particular situation
How fast time passes and the inevitable end it brings
One cannot help but wonder what comes next
What happens when you gasp your last breath

In all the reading I have done, and that's a lot,
I have never found an answer I can accept
For each religion claims that it has got
The answer to that which we each can expect
To find when we finally pass through the gate
And step into the eternity that awaits

Why is it each religion seems to say
That God has spoken through them to all mankind
And that theirs is the one true way
To reach Nirvana leaving all the rest behind
Follow our dogma and tenets and you'll achieve
Paradise forever "Just Believe!"

How can they all be the one true way
If one truly is then all the rest and what they've told
You is wrong and those who believe in what they say
Are doomed for eternity by the dogma they've been sold
Fall not for prophets who will convincingly tell
You the way to avoid eternity in Hell.

I have come to believe beyond a doubt
That God is an invention to answer the need
Of man, who cannot accept that when the lights go out
The movie is over and it's fade to black indeed
When we die there must be some dividend
For all our struggles in a life now at an end

Throughout history religion has played the major part
In creating good and moral ways
Promoting beauty in art, music and the start
Of civilization as we know it today
Alas, religion also has a darker side
Used to promote power with God as the guide

Be not swayed by the siren song of false prophets
Believe in yourself and that little voice in you
That tells you right from wrong and lets
You sleep at night when you do what's right and true
"To thine own self be true" should be your rule
Not becoming some religion's fool

Love Is

Love is warm and love is tender
Love gives no criticism or sting
Love is never the borrower, but the lender
Love is the giver of all things
Love is life and life is love
Love is the one true gift from above

Our Mortality

Death is ever present in our lives
Yet when it strikes a colleague or a friend
The shock is very real and when it arrives
We are not prepared to grasp it is the end

We try to ignore the simple fact that we
Are mortal and inevitably we will die
We know not when that day may be
But it will unavoidably arrive

It is the thing on which religion is founded
That death is not the end, there must be something more
And then when that last bell is sounded
We will pass on to our deserved reward

The clock is ticking fast for us all
Hence enjoy what you have while it is here
Life is a dead end street and death's the wall
And each day it draws ever near

Therefore every day you must make haste
And enjoy the ride while you may
Since tomorrow never comes don't waste
A second, live to the fullest each and every day

What's Next

In my rear view mirror Woodlands fades away into the past
Another phase of my life done and over with for good
Time moves on, things change and nothing lasts
Forever, the good, the bad, all pass, do what you would
The clock ticks on, endless, without cease
So, move on to what comes next with grace and peace

In the fifty-six years that span my working life
I have experienced some most amazing things
Some happy, some sad, some were trouble and strife
Now memories, like snapshots that flash and swing
Across the screen in the theatre of the brain
Renewing the old emotions that remain

At sixteen, with youthful exuberance, I thought I knew it all
At seventy-two I find there is so much more to learn
Too soon old and too late smart always seems to be the call
Experience is a hard teacher, getting your fingers burned
Seems to be the only way to show
Each of us the correct way to go

Now I must embark on a new and challenging career
Defined only by the moods that strike my fancy
One must keep active and go forward without fear
No matter if things seem a little chancy
The moment must be seized before it's gone
"Use it or lose it" now and forever on

Time's Passage

Late August and the dawning comes later every day
The morning mist is thick upon the ground
The animals are foraging for breakfast on their way
The temperature, already warm, is deadening all sounds
The plants make the air sweet and redolent
Everything is fruitful, all life is content.

But as the days are shortening it heralds summer's end
Too soon the frost will coldly rime the earth
The leaves will fall and we will have to contend
With winter's dreary darkness, finding warmth a dearth
The ground will harden and snow will blanket all
Causing life to wither and withdraw.

But as nothing lasts for ever it is also true
For the cold and winter's cruel lament
Spring is around the corner and coming into view
Making way for summer and the warmth's advent
The seasons come and go in an endless stream
All things shall pass away as in a dream.

Love's Fair Favour

I wouldst that thou would come to me
And I to you on bended knee
With arms outstretched in warm embrace
Clasping you thus into a place
Of warmth and love eternally
Entirely saved for you and me.

Two hearts and bodies as one melding
Passion and need in surging motion
Urgency feeding the fires thus welding
Two souls together in love's devotion
I would that this will last forever
Forward, forward ceasing never.

The Joy of Travel

"Getting there is half the fun" is no longer true
For the poor benighted air traveller of today
Instead it is trial by ordeal for anyone who
Dares venture in the modern air terminals forays
A journey not for the faint of heart
A gruelling test right from the start.

It all begins with leaving home with lots of grace
To arrive at the terminal three hours before your flight
Next get your bags and yourself to the check-in place
Pull out your credit card and pay for the right
To take your baggage with you as you travel on
Hoping it will get there too and not go wrong

Then there is the Customs man, who wants to ensure
That you are not up to some nefarious con
Of smuggling contraband or something to injure
The flight that you are taking for your vacation in the sun.
You know that you have nothing, but he does not
And so he has to check all that you've got.

Now that that hurdle has been overcome you spin
On to the next ordeal occurring in the line
Strip your shoes and belt, put your belongings in a bin
Into the metal detector, hoping it will go fine
But knowing it probably won't due to the metal knee
The doctor put in so that you could be pain free.
Sure enough the knee sets off the alarm bells all
So they send you to be wanded and patted down just right
You are poked and prodded up and
down until they make the call
That you are not a threat to anyone on the flight.
Now you are at last free to sit and wait
Until your flight is called up to the departure gate.

At last you struggle down onto the waiting flight
Shuffling along with all the other suffering ones
Squeeze into your seats like sardines in a can so tight
Resting on the tarmac 'til the luggage all is on.
Taxiing to the runway and the take off place
Up, up and away accelerating higher into space.

Finally you're in the air and soaring up so proud
Hastening toward your destination where you hope
To be finished being pressed in with the crowd
And since the worst is over you can begin to cope
With the boredom and cramped quarters that is eased a bit
By watching diversions on your personal screen as you sit.
Once you've landed and you've taxied to the gate
You join the shuffle of passengers off the plane
Now down to baggage claim and start the wait
To get your luggage if it is undamaged in the main.
You're almost there and the goal's in sight
Celebrate, you have survived the fight.

Now outside to try to get a cab going past
And proceed to your resort and start relaxing
Getting there the ordeal is over at last
There are porters there to handle all your things
You now may cheer, your trial is done
Sit back and savour what you've won.

R.I.P.

In quiet repose the dead lie there
Beyond the hustle and the care
Of the living world all around
Peacefully sleeping under ground

Time is not measured by a clock
No news thrills or headlines shock
There are no deadlines, bills to pay
Quietly resting through the days

The history of the city in the graves
Constantly expanding wave on wave
Silent sentinels of things gone by
Proving that time is on the fly

The cemetery is a place for reflection
On things gone by and the realization
That soon you to will fade into the past
And enter the necropolis at last

Life's Meaning

The moments of pleasure are swift and fleeting
Interspersed random flashes in time
But love is a lasting thing, the meeting
Of two souls so mutually entwined

Love is forgiving and caring
Love is warm, a protective shield
Love is a life of giving and sharing
All the good things that life can yield

The flower of love needs constant tending
Lest the weeds of strife start to grow
Nurturing each other, two hearts blending
Will always stay the noxious flow

Together forever in tenderest love
Is truly a gift from heaven above

November

The wind is a bluster of cold through the trees
The empty branches rattle their skeletal fingers
The birds have all fled to the warm southern breeze
The earth lies cold and silent, no life lingers

Soon the January depths will bring forth
Long nights and an icy rime on the ground
Snow driving in on a wind from the north
Not a trace of warmth left to be found

But at the end of winter comes spring
The days grow longer and the sun will shine
The birds will return and the music they bring
Brightens the day, making everything fine

Life will spring forth in a green profusion
The young of the forest cavorting about
Energy erupts, happy at the infusion
Of life as the cycle of the seasons plays out

Life in a Hospital Gown

Hospital gowns, they really are a peach
One size fits all and you cannot demur
They do up the back where you cannot reach
Thus ensuring that exposure will occur

They trot you down a hallway designed to be long
To be sure that a fashion faux pas is bound to befall
When it does they're all "You don't have to worry"
Of course not, it's not them, after all

Hospitals are always kept cool, so you freeze
Since there's large gaps in the gown at play
Once the x-ray is done it's back in the breeze
Down the long hallway, your arse on display

Then in comes the doctor to lift up the gown
And check what it is that is causing the pain
A quick grope and probe which elicits a moan
Then the decision of what treatment to deign

Finally it's all through and you are allowed
To put on your clothes and go home
Going out through the waiting room's crowd
Feeling sorry for the next victim's welcome

Banty Roosters

In the farmers barnyard the Banty rooster struts
He is the smallest and the proudest one of all
The persona he exudes shows that he puts
Himself above all else and all should be in his thrall

It matters not a wit that the truth of it
Is that he doesn't count for very much at all
He puffs out his chest as if he's better than the rest
And doesn't realize that people know he's small

In overcompensating for his personal in securities
He has an ego worthy of someone so much better
But in fact he's so far beneath what he perceives
And everyone realizes he is so much the lesser

Authority Cruelly Used

Have you ever had to work for someone
Who wields their position like a mace
Crushing people just because they can
Making life miserable, it's a disgrace
Destroying people below them, for no gain
It seems they just like inflicting pain.

How miserable their life must be
If the only pleasure they can get
Is harassing people needlessly
How petty and small is their mindset
As they spread their venom far and near
It'll come back one day and bite their rear.

If this should happen to you
Just shrug it off and soldier on
The people who care will stay loyal and true
And be there long after the other is gone
Just do your part and rest assured
That goodness is it's own reward.

As you climb the ladder of fame
Be mindful of those along the way
For sooner or later in the game
They will come back on another day
Remember, what you sow you reap
Life is lonely at the top of the heap.

"UNEASY LIES THE HEAD THAT WEARS THE CROWN"

Shakespeare "Henry the Fourth"

Ad Nauseum

Snivelling grovelling sycophants are a nauseating crew
Their bussing authority's derrieres is a sight to behold
If the boss stops quick they get a whiplash and a bruise
Their constant lip service is a story to be told

They have no shame and no remorse, they grovel endlessly
Their nose so far up you wonder how they breathe
Agreeing with everything that's said indubitably
It's enough to give a person the spontaneous dry heaves

It makes one wonder why these bosses put up with it
Don't they see it for what it is, a false friend
Flattery to get ahead, all so much bullshit
Yet these sycophants seem to get what they want in the end

Perhaps it's nature's way of evening everything out
Punishment for the people who get ahead by foul means or fair
To have no one around them but these fawning louts
Makes for an empty life with nothing there

In the Afterglow

The moment of the rain and clouds subsides
The tender lasting glow now remains
The warmth of love now resides
In the encompassing embracing refrain
Of two hearts and souls entwined
Eternally one to the end of time.

Love that lasts is not born of lust
But of respect and desire and hope
That, together joined in trust
Through life's journey the two can cope
Being united, two people melded
In one Karma, solidly welded.

Personal Strength

The fog of self-doubt and of confusion
Clouds the mind and eats away at the soul
It corrodes the spirit and creates the delusion
Of your being a lesser person in the whole

Trust in yourself and you will find
That peace and contentment will surely follow
Confidence builds on itself in the mind
Leading you on to satisfying tomorrows

Success and failure are transitory things
Each shall in their turn pass by
Accept what comes as each day brings
On new challenges for you to try

Unbidden Things

How convoluted are life's ways
The things that change the path of our feet
The subtle things that alter the day
From the way we thought to meet
The plan we had laid out before
For the successful completion of our chores

The broken shoelace that caused the delay
Of five minutes and hence you were where
You would not have been on a normal day
So when the accident happened, you were there
Happenstance unexpectedly brings
A change to the order daily things

So ever it goes, just random chance
That brings on changes we would not have made
An unplanned meeting blooming into romance
The discovery that convinces you to trade
This for that, a sudden swing
From left to right and all that brings

These things unplanned morph our life's shape
Our best laid plans fall by the way
A new plan becomes necessary to create
A viable map of the brand new way
Flexibility is needed for you to cope
With the inevitable alteration of your hopes

John Lennon said

"LIFE IS WHAT HAPPENS TO YOU WHILE YOU'RE PLANNING FOR SOMETHING ELSE"

Joie de Vivre

The sun is like a warm arm across the shoulders
The breeze caresses the cheek like a lover's lips
The sunlight dapples the moss covered boulders
Calmness spreads outward to the finger tips

Small animals darting to and fro amongst the brush
Bird's songs fill the tree tops with happy sound
The air is redolent with scent of the blooming blush
Life is springing forth profusely all around

Moments such as this are to be treasured
The thrill of life courses through the veins
Nothing is needed to complete the pleasure
The senses are replete and joy is sustained
To share this time with one that you hold dear
Can truly bring Nirvana very near

The Times of Janus

The Romans had a god who had two faces
One that looked forward and one that faced back
So it is in life as things keep changing places
One phase ends and another starts it's track

One can't keep looking backward, thusly missing what's ahead
You can't live in the past as time does not stand still
You must keep moving forward and stay steady in your tread
Lest stagnation sets in and kills ambition's will

Remembering times gone by surely warms the heart
Harbouring old grudges is a crushing weight
Lay aside old hurts and push forward to the start
Of a new day and the future's beckoning gate
Live on in hope and confidence and happiness will follow
Gaining new successes and a great tomorrow

In Each Other

Weather heightens passion no matter what the season
In winter's bleakest moments or in summer's heat
The closeness of a lover will always provide the reason
For the arousal and the quickening of the beat
One never knows when or what will spark the fire
Centered on the one your heart most desires

In winter cuddled up so warm and near
Passion will automatically ensue
In summer when the warmth is here
Outdoors in a wooded setting arouses you
The only thing dictated by the weather
Is the location of your get together

Revel in the joy of your love's blessing
Keep the embers of it burning bright
Gentle warmth, not lust, should fan your caressing
For love to continue to emit the guiding light
The giving of love is the lasting thing
That the joy of each other will always bring

Egocentric Oafs

People mistake money for breeding and class
Hence the rich over inflate their social status
When the truth is, mostly they are just crass
Not understanding their place in hierarchal caucus
Through inheritance, or connivance, or happenstance
They've acquired their wealth and high circumstance

Pelf does not make them honest or strong
Number forty-five is living proof in part
What they need is a sense of right and wrong
Social responsibility, a conscience, a heart
The courage and strength to do what is right
Not take the easy way out of a fight

To help those in need with no thought of reward
Forgiving and kind to those who've done wrong
A leg up to one who's luck's gone by the board
Sharing your good fortune to bring them along
These are the things that show style and grace
And make you a winner in life's chase

Unfortunately, most wealthy do not feel the need
To fulfill the social responsibility their status brings
Instead their main thrust is self-interest and greed
A sense of entitlement to everything
Devil take the hindmost, I'll be fine
You'll not get a share of what is mine

The more they get, the more they strive
Chiselling, cheating, exploiting every contest
Sparing no one and nothing in their drive
To accumulate more in their endless quest
"Til they finally see the grave's gaping stare
Their power and wealth means nothing there

All that they achieved will be swept away
Nothing will last for posterity
No one to mourn, no glowing eulogies play
A life swallowed up by eternity
Nothing to show for that conniving life
Just a legacy of trouble and strife

The First Day of the Rest of Your Life

Of late I have been thinking that all my tomorrows are past
And that there is actually very little left in the hour glass
But today it came to me that while this may be true
I must make the best of what is left before I'm through.

Since this is the very first day of the rest of my life
I will try to make the best of each moment that goes by
Try and do all those things I have been leaving by the way
Endeavour to cross something off the bucket list without delay.

My main concern, which is also the easiest to do
Is to get down all the rhymes I've
thought of as time quickly flew
By me at a breakneck speed unnoticed as it passed
Until at last I'm staring at an almost empty glass.

Cast off old angers, sins and wrongs, insults, bad debts unpaid
They only weigh you down and erode
any pleasure left to be made
Take each day as fresh and new, enjoy the little things
Drink deeply of each moment and the pleasure that it brings.

Ideal Fulfilled

Her soulful eyes are large and dark and cool
Mysterious in their depth and pleasure
Shining they draw you into fathomless pools
A fantasy of love and endless treasure.

Her velvet skin and long dark hair
Cupid's bow lips and dimpled cheek
A hint of a smile that's lurking there
A promise of the things you seek.

Fulfillment comes when you finally touch
The warmth, the glow of a love completed
The soft tender kiss long desired so much
Gives the sense of a heart fully repleted.

Not fiery heat of lust and passion
But the gentle satisfaction of joining hearts
The lasting affection formed in the fashion
Of love meant to be right from the start.

Mandatory Attendance

City Hall in it's infinite wisdom has deigned
That any employee who should have a slip
In a city vehicle resulting in a traffic claim
Shall receive a re-training program removing the blip
From the driver's consciousness, correcting the error
Thus diminishing the public's traffic terror.

Gathered in a room that's been prepared
With seats and a screen for the presentation
Of defensive driving, with nothing spared
To ensure the complete re-education
Of the offending miscreant
To become a more productive public servant.

The lecture drones and the eyelids droop
The mind wanders and time drags by
But, surprisingly, some information is scooped
And the learning curve does actually rise
The experience truly does, in the end,
Pay off with some helpful dividends.

It is always a good day when something is learned
Helpful hints that will make you more aware
And a better driver who has turned
Into one who will take greater care
Of the way you handle the day to day
As you travel and drive along your way.

Fulfillment

The dimple in the cheek and the twinkle in the eye
The enticement of lips begging to be kissed
The softness of the cheek when it's touching mine
All make for such a culminating bliss
That life's delight is there for me to take
She is the only wish that I would make.

Her presence is all I need to gain paradise
The sound of her voice is music to my ears
To feel her body next to mine completes the rise
Of all my hopes and dreams, removing fears
From such a stuff as this am I replete
There's nothing else on earth that can compete.

Internal Strife

Civic management is about as poorly run
As any place could ever be
Ask anyone who has had the fun
Of dealing with the bureaucracy
Those gray faceless office pogues who
Will mindlessly recite the rules for you

The management team yearly come around
With a donut, a cup of coffee and a smile
And tell the workers on the ground
How great they are, when all the while
They don't know you or really care
You wonder why they're even there

The people they place in command
Are arrogant, abrasive and not all that bright
Or else they would truly understand
Leadership is not about having might
The harder you push, the more resistance you meet
Hence their methods themselves defeat

The system perpetuates itself ever on
The ineffectual methods stay after the cretins leave
The evil that they do lives on after they're gone
And when new men try to relieve
The situation they are crushed into submission
Removing any chance of completing their mission

They talk about changing and improving the culture
And then continue on in the same old vein
Thusly ensuring that the future
Will only be the caboose of the same train
They don't learn from past mistakes and trips
But carry forward the same old ways and slips

History repeats itself is an old adage
That over and over seem to prove it's true
But the people in charge seem to manage
To overlook this in their point of view
Thus continuing on blindly to defeat
Their own efforts as history once more repeats

Albert Einstein said:

"INSANITY IS DOING THE SAME THING OVER AND OVER AND EXPECTING A DIFFERENT RESULT"

A Winter Moment

Silent soft the snow is sifting
Cloaking the world in purest white
Deadening sounds, no noises drifting
No imperfections are in sight

All too soon the world intrudes
Into the calm and peaceful scene
But, for now, serenity rules
A moment to enjoy and be replete

Even in winter's darkest days
If you look you can find pleasure
Taking things as they come your way
Gives happiness that you can treasure

Darwinism

Man has forever asked "Why are we here"
Who planned this marvelous universe so rife
And there's always someone standing near
To give us the answer to the riddle of life.

There must be some magnificent power in sway
To design so intricate a scheme
To work in such an interlocking way
Each thing in it's place in this web-like theme.

Surely God must be all powerfully intelligent
To get things to run in the way that they do
No detail is too small to miss his bent
The master plan is working through and through.

Everyone seems to be missing the evolutionary effect
What about the species that were here at the start
Were they just mistakes that should be expected
In the giant experiment of which we are part.

I believe the plain and simple truth about
It is it simply worked out this way
And is still evolving, spinning out
Moving on to a new and different day.

Our belief that we are the culmination
Of everything and we are the peak
Of this giant experiment in evolution
Is simply our human egotistical cheek.

Long eons ago the tiny mammal arose
Outlasting the dinosaurs and winning the race
When the day of man draws to a close
What species will arise to take our place.

Throughout Earth's history there have been
Many species that have come and gone
Nothing lasts for ever as we have seen
And soon our turn will be done.

Dealing with Life

A bird flying overhead with flapping wings
The wind carries the bird along by chance
Seeming to presage the randomness that life brings
Maybe to danger, maybe romance
Success and failure are fleeting, fast
Disappearing quickly into the past

Dwell not on what has gone before
Look ahead to what comes next
Time has a way of evening the score
When taken in the long context
Stride on with purpose, bold and strong
Savouring each new thing that comes along

To waste your time on petty strife
Trying to get even for perceived wrongs
Only wastes some more of your life
That should be spent in moving on
To more constructive and happier things
And the satisfaction which they bring

Autumnal Equinox

The wind cuts like a knife as it blows the leaves around
The dampness in the air causes the joints to complain
The day is the colour of ditch water and propounds
The coming of drear winter as the seasons change

But, just as summer is gone, so too will winter follow
All things change regularly in their turn
As certain as the dawning of tomorrow
Spring will come heralding the return
Of warmth and life and hope and future happiness
And all the things that the summer's seasons bless

CHAPTER FOUR

Consequences

Consequences

The snarling lips of hate curled back
The dripping fangs of revenge uncovered
The burning eyes of bigotry lack
The ability to accept differences of others
Believing theirs is the one true way
Brings out the beast of fanaticism
Until cruelty becomes the norm of the day
The unlettered brutish catechism
Evil feeds upon itself growing ever bigger
In a downward spiral into the abyss
Reason is abandoned, violence is triggered
Human values gone badly amiss
Until it all crashes in a cataclysmic convulsion
Of fear and anger and revulsion

When the orgy of hate and violence abates
Drowned in a sea of blood and waste
The fingers of blame anxiously await
Pointed by each at the other in haste
Saying that they were not part of the crime
Just innocent bystanders caught in the moment
In the wrong place at the wrong time
Surrounded by all the rioting foment

When the time comes to pay the bill
No one will step up and take the blame
It's all passing the buck around until
All are tarred with the brush of shame

The lesson never seems to be learned
Just shelved until the next eruption burns

Evening's Blessing

The sun is setting in the west, giving the sky an orange hue
Sitting in the gloaming with our hands entwined
The warmth of the moment shared being next to you
Brings forth an emotion too strong to be defined
Would that this moment could but last forever
Two souls as one enmeshed in love together.

Hamilton Civic Cemeteries

In the City of Hamilton there are sixty-seven
Places of repose, Civic Cemeteries
Where reside the remains of the men and women
Who have played a role making this City
The pleasant place we see before us today
They each of them had a role to play.

No matter how insignificant or small
Or starring in a leading place in time
They all contributed, a brick in the wall
That made Hamilton into the prime
And wonderful place it has grown to be
A place to live and grow, and that's the key.

The oldest of the cemeteries are a record in stone
Of the founding fathers, how it all began
The struggles of the settlers starting out alone
In a wilderness untouched by the hand of man.
Wresting a hard living from the uncleared earth
Toiling from morn 'til night to fill their dearth.

As the city grew from its humble start
So the need for cemeteries, to inter the dead
Thus the Civic Cemeteries were born, and their part
In recording the passage of time as it fled
On towards the future, where we stand today
Preserving what we've gathered along the way.

People rarely think in their daily story
Of the past and how things came to be this way
But, in the cemetery it's all about memory
A history lesson each and every day.
Those that do not learn from the past
Are doomed to repeat those mistakes aghast.

Hamilton is fortunate in that they
Have cemeteries run by management who care
About the bereaved and seek to stay
A part of the sorrow of the family there.
Trying to relieve the anguish and the pain
Of the lost loved one they'll never see again.

For those who are familiar with local history
There are some names most worthy of note
On the stones as you make your foray
Into the sections, row by row.
All the people of the years gone by
Showing time is ever on the fly.

Christ's Church and the Church of the Ascension
Started using "The Heights" as a burial ground
About 1850, with each having a section
Now on the south side, where can be found
Names you will recognize, but not know the story
Of the people there, now gone to glory.

The Gatehouse Lodge at the main road
Was completed about 1862
Originally a chapel and the abode
Of the Caretaker, but later grew
Into the main office and also afford
A repository for Civic Cemetery records.

The Office Staff are there to provide
Information to people who need assistance
In arranging a funeral and decide
The best location for their individual instance
Helping them in their time of sorrow
Navigating through to a new tomorrow.

Management has the most difficult task
Of answering everyone's particular needs
Clients who consistently ask
For accommodation of their own creeds
While not interfering with the others there
Causing older clients more worry and care.

The grounds keeping staff have the burden
Of interring the people day to day
And keeping the parklike areas verdant
Stopping the encroachment of things unstayed
Making the cemeteries a place of reflection
And repose, away from life's interjections.

As people pass, or enter the gates
Of the cemeteries, they should reflect
On the passage of time and the fate
That awaits us all, as death comes to collect.
Sooner or later we all shall be
Another small part of Hamilton's history.

Conflict from Confusion

Most disputes arise from misreading words and signs
By people hearing what they want to hear
Or imparting meaning that was not the intent
Of the other person's conversational bent.

It also comes from saying what you think they want to hear
Instead of what you truly want or feel
Since the listener will not necessarily react in the way
That the speaker was hoping for on this particular day.

Obfuscation, blowing smoke and misdirecting messages
Will cause frustration and irascibility
Placing one's cards openly and honestly on the table
Can cool things down and make life more reasonable.

It will not always solve your differences but,
At least you both will know where you each stand
Instead of wasting time and energy on pretenses
Try putting all your effort into mending fences.

Let not old hurts and wrongs cloud your mind
Slough off all of the past and let it lie
Move forward with hope and freshness in your heart
Keeping your intended goal as the only prize.

Controlling Fate

When you have the feeling that things are beyond your control
Making you feel that you are a puppet on a string
Each time you turn around there is a new stone for you to roll
Up the hill of Sisyphus to stem the next disastrous thing

Sometimes things seem to cartwheel of their own accord
Happenstance can often leave you staring and aghast
Trying to keep abreast of it can very well have you floored
So step back and take a breath because this will not last

Take heart, for as in all things, this too shall soon end
And the storm clouds of trouble will surely clear away
Accept things as they come and just around the bend
The sun will shine again on a brand new day

Never let it get you down, just stay the course
Keep on swimming and the tide will turn
And don't forget that it could always be much worse
So chin up and carry on with another lesson learned

Elocution of Love

The tip of the tongue, the teeth, the lips
Make speech and love the very best
The whispered word in the ear that trips
The heat of desire leading to a caress
Of the skin with lips brushing, arousing
The nerve ends for the tongue's carousing.

Gentle kisses and nips of the teeth, just right
Fingers touching, feeling and exploring
Make loving a thing of pure delight
With affection and wantonness now outpouring
The joy of giving and receiving love
Is truly a gift from the heavens above

A Breathing Space

When anger is the driving force that rules your life
Everything will end up in arguing and strife
Nothing will go forward in a positive mode
Trouble and sadness will only pave your road.

Staying your anger for a breathing space
Slowing the pulse that reddens the face
Everything will ease and let reason take hold
Before pride starts to rule and trouble enfolds.

All have a chance to take a thoughtful step back
Instead of leaping to the snarling attack
And then as cooler heads start to prevail
Compromise is easier and soothes the travails.

The theory is simple but the reality is not
To quell the anger when the moment gets hot
But with thought and practice you will gain
The habit of calmness that you can sustain.

Connections

The warmth of love nurtures the soul
From a friend or from a husband or wife
It makes both the giver and taker whole
And without it there is an emptiness to life

To find someone with whom you can connect
Brings a joy that words cannot define
And when the feeling is returned in kind
It is a satisfaction that is almost perfect

Friendship, love and amity always bring
To your life a happiness that can't be bought
Thus when you find it your heart will sing
Songs that only warm emotions could have wrought

Be Thankful for the Moment

As the season changes with the hour glass sands
The thought occurs that we don't appreciate
That which we have before us in our hand
Taking so much for granted until it's too late

Only once does our child say its first word
Only once is it your first anniversary
Only once can your apology be heard
With the meaning it was meant to say

Each day is a gift, so treat it as such
Relish the good with gratitude and thanks
Hold close the loved ones that mean so much
Cherish each moment in a memory bank

Far too soon the moments gone
Never more to come again
Once it's passed your chance is done
And it will never return in that vein

Try to make the most of what you receive
Worry not on what has gone by
Look ahead, on the past don't grieve
Absorb each experience, time's on the fly

Be My Valentine

In all the years that we have been together
The attraction has not dimmed nor lost it's charm
Through all the good times and the stormy weather
I still need you there beside me on my arm.
Without you I would not be complete
You are the one that makes my soul replete.

Alternate Realities

Time bends and the lines blur
Right and wrong is altered
'Til feathers now become fur
And the upright falter
And then are morphed into
A mutant shaped thing
Unfamiliar to you
The confusion it brings
Clouds the mind
So let your inner voice
Stay strong and hold sway
And make the moral choice
Which will save the day
Shades of gray fall away
The truth will break through
The sun shines and the sky is blue.

June 6th, 1944

Tuesday June 6th 1944
The like of which no one had ever seen
Or likely ever will again

In the first twenty-four hours
150,000 men landed on the coast
Of Normandy in France

Fortress Europa's days were numbered

4,413 young men of various nations
Paid the ultimate price
To gain a foothold on the Nazi occupied continent

The date was set for June 5th
But a summer gale postponed it
Tides and the moon were only right
For the next two days

General D. D. Eisenhower bit the bullet
And made the call
GO!
And it was on

It began twenty four hours earlier
With blanket bombing of strategic targets

French Resistance played havoc with German logistics
Railroads, highways, communications

Paratroopers were dropped in hours before the landings
Causing confusion and mayhem behind the coast
Miles off shore titanic battleships pounded coastal defenses
Each shell weighed approximately one ton
Closer in shore cruisers and destroyers added to the cacophony
Of death and destruction

Amazingly most bunkers and defenders
Survived these initial barrages
They set up their machineguns and mortars
And prepared for the landings about to ensue

Soldiers climbed down the scramble nets into the waiting
Landing craft tossing and heaving in the channel waters
And began the long journey in to the hostile beaches

The craft hit the beach
The ramp dropped
The first casualty
Hit in the forehead, dead before he knew it

Men splashing ashore in a hail of bullets
Fate indiscriminately killing one
Wounding one
Missing one
Don't stop for your mate
Keep moving or become a casualty yourself

Men huddled in the dunes
Trying to survive

Men stepping up and taking charge
"Move out or die where you are"
Didn't leave much choice

Then came moments of selfless heroism
Rushing forward, ignoring bullets
Forget the consequences
Only thought to put a grenade in that pillbox
And stop the slaughter of men
Pinned in the dunes

Countless men doing daring deeds
Unnoticed except by those men they saved
Many paying with their lives
To do the deed that no one else would dare
But by their actions, enough survived to carry the day!

Once they had a foothold on the beaches
It was just a matter of time before
Victory so long sought after came.

Now those beaches where young men
Fought and died are empty
Save for vacationers frolicking in the surf
Sword, Gold, Juno, Omaha, Utah
Are now just names in a history book
With Thermopylae, Trafalgar, Vimy Ridge
Again I say
They were called, and they answered
They gave their all
We owe them much

On Remembrance Day think on them and be grateful

Unrealistic Views

I am sure at some time you have met
That person who always seems to know better
Than everyone else in a given set
Insisting that his way be followed to the letter
Becoming as annoying as he can get
Thus complicating what was a simple matter.

Before too long they have elbowed their way
To the fore pushing everyone back aghast
Never listening, just talking, an endless spray
Of information on how in their past
It was always done this way
'Til everyone else just drifts aside at last.

"Never argue with a fool" it's said
Because before so very long
You start to sound like him, instead
Of singing your own particular song
At last it pops into your head
"I'm becoming him" and that is wrong.

Unsolicited advice is like feces.
Everybody's got some, but nobody else wants it!

Amor in Aeternum

The touch of the fingertips that electrifies the senses
The brush of the lips that brings forth the flush
The warmth of the embrace that further enhances
The emotional storm that comes in a rush.
It all peaks together in a culminating burst
Releasing the buildup of love's burning thirst.

But the best of it all is the residual glow
That fulfils the heart and feeds the soul
Proving love outlasts lust and ever grows
Long after passion recedes to a smouldering coal.
The love that sustains us and nurtures the heart
Will be there forever, the lingering part.

Toxic People

There are people in this world who's life is spent
In one constant disapproving sneer
Finding fault and placing blame is their sole intent
It seems the only reason they are here
It's as if the only pleasure they can get
Is in degrading anything they've met

They can find an insult in the coming dawn
Everything to them is a put down or a slur
They will never concede a point in anything they're on
Me, me, me is all they want to hear
Their inability to see things in a true light
Blinds them to the truth and to the right

The space around these people is always filled
With tension and underlying angry feelings
Their persecution complex will not be stilled
The pettiness of it all will send you reeling
There is no up side to these toxic ones
The world is all the colder 'til their time is done

Noel

Christmas is a special time of year
With mixed emotions both sweet and sad,
Causing one to shed a silent tear
For loved ones who are no longer here.

Remembering Christmases of my youth
With grandparents, parents and family dear
So warm to remember but the truth
Of their absence will evoke a tear

Creating new memories with the young
For them to recall in future days
Softens the sorrow that was begun
When thinking back to your youthful ways.

Too soon time will have passed away
And you will be the absent one now gone
They will look back to the olden days
Memories to which they are drawn.

New Year

Another year came and went
Into time's endless stream
Weaving the fabric of the past
With no edge of a seam
Eternally on the flow moves fast
Relentless in it's bent.

Some of the deeds were done
And some were left behind
To gather dust upon a shelf
Left forgotten out of mind
In our endless quest for pelf
For trophies of battles won.

By the time that we have won
That which we most dearly sought
And strove in the flames of desire
We find out that what we've bought
Does not quench the fire
But only spurs us ever on.

Take heart and look forward in the mist
Life's joy is not in the prize
But in the journey of the quest
And strength you gain with your tries
Satisfaction in doing your best
'Til the brass ring is in your fist.

Nature's Lesson

The gentle kissing of the wavelets on the sand
A slow, soft on-shore breeze on the blow
The warmth of the sun beaming down on the land
All combining together to make the heart glow
Ah, would that this moment could last forever
Perpetually onward, ceasing never.

Life by the sea is a marvellous thing
Whether summer, winter, autumn or spring
Each season with the wonders that they bring,
The might of the gale, the howl of the storm
Picking up pieces of detritus the next morn
Stoic determination with which it is borne.

All That I desire

Her lips are made for kissing and for words of love
Her eyes are alluring and promise heaven on earth
Her warmth is a blessing, paradise enough
To satisfy my cravings and fulfill my dearth
She is my goddess and she makes my life replete
Making all of my fantasies complete.

Move Ever Forward

Look to the future, ever forward, never back
Learn from the past but do not dwell
On past hurts or slights, that's not the tack
The past cannot be changed, you can't unring the bell.

Spend your time in positive pursuits
Grow your heart and mind in learning ways
Let kind and helpful things be the fruit
Of the tree of your life throughout your days.

Anger, hatred, revenge just waste your time
When you could be enjoying growth and calm
Defeat and failure are corrosive climes
Love and friendship are a healing balm.

Go forth in calm and serenity embrace
And the sun shall forever warm your face.

All I Have to Give

My one real wish is that I could do
Whatever it takes to ensure
All my love's wishes would come true
Be ever ready to do more
In making her life complete
And that all her desires are replete.

The happiness in her face
Is always my greatest reward
Nothing could ever replace
Her appreciation in that regard
Her love is my greatest treasure
Her happiness my greatest pleasure.

May's Promise

In the early May
As dawns the day
Comes the promise of new life that's best
The buds are busy greening
And the birds are preening
To attract a mate and build a nest.

All the people seem too
To be refreshed anew
With the promise of the summer yet to come
Dead winter's cruel cold
Is dispelled by the golden
Warmth of the strengthening sun.

Eternally up hope springs
And then the heart sings
With the coming of all the new life
All thoughts will now turn
And the passions burn
At the end of winter's lengthy strife.

With thoughts on the morrow
And all the joy to follow
Summer stretches out ahead in endless days
The frolic and the fun
Which has only just begun
Life is beautiful and good in every way.

Obsessive Compulsive

Have you ever met someone so totally obsessed
With directing everything and everyone around
Correcting, cajoling, until everyone's so stressed
And nothing can escape the awful sound
Of that harsh and strident voice
That never gives anyone a choice.

If just once they'd shut their trap
Letting all the rest have a break
Instead of the constant yap
Think of the progress you could make.
Ah, would that it were ever so
But sadly that's just not how it goes.

Canada at Vimy Ridge

An escarpment lying south east of Arras
Was captured by the Germans in 1914
Giving them the ability to harass
All the countryside that could be seen
From the crest of the ridge and thus prevent
Any counter attack the Entente could present

By 1916 the war had bogged down and became
A stalled, static, trench war full of artillery duels
A war of attrition with no end to the game
As countless men were fed into hungry mill
Generals thinking if they just sent in more men
The corner could be turned and bring on the end

The Canadian Army was still in its infancy
An untried force from the colonies
Mixed in piecemeal to the general foray
Of the melting pot of the British Army
Not a separate entity on its own
Untried and generally unknown

The French Army was planning a major push for a decision
General Nivelle asked the British Army to assist
With a diversionary battle at the Vimy Ridge position
Thus drawing off German assets being used to resist
Hoping this would bring about the break out they'd need
In order for the Entente's efforts to succeed

General Haig agreed and the decision was made
General Currie said Canada could accomplish the task
But only if they agreed to do it his way
With four Canadian Divisions, all together at last
He prepared in innovative ways with great care
To ensure that a solid victory would be theirs

On March the 5th 1917 the plan was approved
The drilling and practice began and was thorough
The Artillery was in place and the last obstacles removed
With every last shell they could beg, steal or borrow
The date, Easter Sunday, April 8th was finally set
But postponed twenty-four hours at the French Army's request

At 5:30 am on Monday April ninth the attack was begun
A snow storm was blowing in the faces of those defending
A creeping barrage lead the way, bringing the attackers along
To the German positions that now needed contending
And now began the hand to hand struggle in the trenches
As the Canadians dropped into the German's firing benches

The fighting continued through two days and two nights
'Til finally around six PM on the twelfth it was done
All around the dead were piled, a most horrific sight
Now came the tallying of the cost of the battle we had won
Three thousand six hundred of Canada's youth had perished
To win this great battle that we now all cherish

Seven thousand men wounded also added to the butcher's bill
Of the pain and the suffering the young men had to endure
To gain the crest of bloody Vimy Ridge and instill
In all Canadians a national pride not known before
The cost was high but Canada showed on the world's stage
A proud young country that had come of age

The country called and these young men did not shrink
"Ready, aye ready" for the fray, forget the cost
Going overseas to France and stand on the brink
Of manmade hell on earth and then get tossed
Into the maelstrom of the battle's hell
Doing brave deeds and winning out so well

They were not special or unordinary when they came
The heat of battle hardened them in the fight
Most of them unknown and unnamed
Yet they stepped up when others shrank in fright
We owe them much, they gave their all and more
Remember them and be grateful for their gift of yore

Laurence Binyon said:

"THEY SHALL NOT GROW OLD AS WE THAT ARE LEFT GROW OLD AGE SHALL NOT WEARY THEM, NOR THE YEARS CONDEMN AT THE GOING DOWN OF THE SUN AND IN THE MORNING WE WILL REMEMBER THEM"

Maintaining Calm

There are certain times in life
When the trouble and the strife
Will seem as though it's never going to end
And the people all around you
Relentlessly hound you
And drive you to distraction 'round the bend.

You must gather up your strength
And go to any length
To marshal your resources as you go
So when they do their worst
And you feel you're going to burst
Don't ever let your inner feelings show.

Be sure you don't let slip
And don't ever lose your grip
And rage and scream at your most ardent foes
Because that will only show
That your reeling from their blows
And they'll get satisfaction at your throes.

The calm that you maintain
Will dampen all their pains
To make you lose your smooth and even keel
Don't give them a chance to gloat
As they're tearing at your throat
Grin and bear it and don't show how you feel.

Loved Ones

Loneliness is a cancer that eats away at the soul
It debilitates and drains your very being
A heart needs companionship to be completely whole
To share in everything you're doing and seeing.

Sharing is as necessary as the food we eat
It is the reason to awake each day
The warmth and affection helps us to meet
The trials and turmoil that we face each day.

Sharing an accomplishment with someone whom
Is near and dear makes the victory complete
A shoulder to lean on when failure or trouble loom
Softens the blow and the sting of defeat.

Appreciate the persons who you hold very dear
Whether a spouse, a sibling, or a friend
They are the ones that you must keep so near
And sustain them to the very end.

Adoration

My life is filled beyond repletion
With a love that burns ever bright
For the woman who makes my completion
My Goddess and my guiding light
To worship at her body's altar
Is my one desire that never falters.

Looking Ahead

The old year fades slowly into the past
The new year stretches out ahead
Time flits by, it seems so fast
The future looms full of hope and dread

Will tomorrow be just more of the same
There's a lot to be said for consistency
But better days are what we hope to claim
In the next scene of posterity

The future is yours to make as you please
To go forward in hope to greener fields
Let old grudges and anger cease
Work at the good that the new year yields

Life's Storms

The air is thick and heavy underneath a glowering sky
The driving wind is causing the thunder clouds to fly
A storm is in the offing, you can feel it if you try
The tossing of the leaves heralds the tempest drawing nigh

When the storm finally bursts it's almost a relief
We can weather it should be our constant belief
And so it is in life as we suffer through disaster
"We can weather it" should always be your answer

Life to the Fullest

The closer to the end, the brighter should your light burn
Desperately try to squeeze out every last drop
That life has to offer before that last inevitable turn
That brings on the final curtain and full stop
From which there is no coming back again
Just stillness, fade to black, the show's complete
Gone to the past where it will remain
A dusty footnote in time's ceaseless beat
Everything is so fleeting and transitory
Great deeds and small will all soon pass away
Hence enjoy what's here before you pass to glory
Live each day as if it were your last
Don't blink because it all passes by so fast

Leadership

Leadership is an ephemeral thing
Sought by many, but achieved by few
The concept is not easily brought
Out in a person with no charisma who
Wishes to lead but cannot inspire
The wish to please that loyalty requires

Power and authority cannot guarantee
That people will eagerly respond to you
Charisma is that something that people see
And makes them eager and willing to
Follow your lead anywhere
Do any task that you prepare

Authority backed up by the whip
Will accomplish things, but always fails
To evoke great deeds or prevent the slip
Into the lack lustre performance servility entails
Only leadership can truly bring into view
The inspiration to do great things for you

It Matters not

The winds of Fate are blowing capriciously about
Storm clouds of doubt and turmoil fill the sky
It is a time of question and one cannot doubt
That uncertainty is rife and time is on the fly

The wheel of fortune spins, some will win and some will lose
To the victor go the spoils is ever true
But the truth of it is no matter which one the Gods do choose
This too shall pass as time moves on
and turns to something new

Worry not on things that you cannot change
What will happen, will happen no matter what
Relax and enjoy the ride as the scene is rearranged
And remember to enjoy all that you've got

Irrelevance

As retirement looms and time moves forward
I find myself looking at and seeing
A time with nothing to look toward
Except sitting and watching the world being
Carried on by people doing the things
That having a purpose in life brings

Retirement relegates you to the sidelines
To sit and observe, not participate
Left, discarded, out of sight and out of mind
No one cares if you're early or late
Nobody wants or listens to your thoughts
Or the wisdom that experience has brought

You must have a reason to arise each day
Look to yourself for your motivation to
Try to accomplish something along the way
Of the rest of your life, don't waste time just do
All you can and you will discover that
"Life's for the living" is where it's at

Inanity

A conversation in a group develops out of hand
And the ebb and flow will take it where it will
Until someone injects some lunacy to the brand
Then it's all downhill from there and stupidity fills
The air like a miasmatic plague
Making logic and good sense seem very vague

There is a saying that goes "never argue with a fool"
Because before too long has passed you will find
Inanity breeds inanity is the abiding rule
You will begin to answer in the same kind.
Be careful how and when you have your say
Lest you degenerate downward in the selfsame way.

In Order to Succeed

The worms of doubt eat through your brain
The shadows of fear fill your thoughts
Hesitation threatens to derail the train
Of success, the wonder that you've wrought

Last night it all seemed so sound and wise
The morning's harsh light blurs the lines
The model in the mind shrinks in size
Until it almost vanishes in decline

Do not lose faith in your original aim
Square up and cast aside all of your doubts
Rectify the flaws that seem to claim
The intent of what your plan was all about

Courage, fortitude, and not losing sight
Of the brass ring that's within your span
Will get you past all of the frights
To where success is in your hand

Impending End

By the side of life's road the old man sits
And waits as time slides by
Worn out and tired by all the hits
Of life received, he looks misty eyed
Back to a time when he was young
And the world was fresh and new
Back when the day had just begun
Oh Damn! but that time just flew

Now no one waits for his return
His wife, now dead, and children grown
No candle in the window burns
To guide his feet on their way home
Alone, bereft, friends all dead
He sits and watches with a bowed head

All that is left is the final scene
When the Reaper comes to collect his due
The cold embrace that will mean
He is finally passing through
That one way gate and join with they
Who have already gone to pave the way

Fanciful Fears

Out of the dark the night sweats come
Fear creeps in on padded feet
Irrational thoughts that spring from
Unseen things that flap and beat
Out of reach at the edge of our senses
Leaving us vulnerable and defenseless.

Strange sounds that in the dark
Stir the imagination to a fever pitch
Cats that yowl and dogs that bark
Rouse old fears of demons and witches
When daylight comes reality steps in
We think of our fears with a red faced grin.

Worry yourself not on imagined things
Believe in what you can feel and touch
The only thing that darkness brings
Is a time for rest that you need so much
So relax and rest in an easy way
To repair yourself for another day.

Equanimity

After reading the Confucian Analects it occurred to me
That I needed more balance and less stress in my life
So I made a conscious decision to reduce the aggression
And not let anger be my first reaction to strife.

In our everyday existence we meet with resistance
And the constant jockeying for everything that's nigh
From the gridlocked streets to the line-ups that we meet
Whilst trying to get a cup of coffee on the fly.

We see it all the time in every race and clime
People that will constantly push to the fore
It matters not a whit because the truth of it
Is it doesn't really get you anything more.

All the pushing and the shoving actually gains you nothing
Since you wind up in the same place anyway
The bobbing and the weaving and the pulling and the heaving
Leave you only two minutes ahead for all your play.

So now I'm going to try to achieve before I die
A philosophical equanimity
Thusly enjoying a lot more of the time that I have got
Left before I slip into eternity.

Emotions

For better or for worse, emotions control our actions
And they run hot and high when out of control
When managed properly they can bring satisfaction
When not, they play a very destructive role.

Anger leads to rashness and bad options
Hatred leads to bitterness and remorse
Lust leads to excess and dissipation
Greed leads to meanness and discord.

Love leads to warmth and charity
Kindness leads to happiness and charm
Temperance leads to calmness and serenity
Building a life that conflict cannot harm.

Foster all of your positive emotions
Control the negative reactions and at length
Calmness will steady all the bustle and commotion
Temperance will conquer all the bad with strength.

Passage of Time

Think of life as an hour glass
Sands moving ceaselessly on
Each grain is a moment that passes
Quickly, so quickly, then gone
Into the void of the past
Nothing ever really lasts.

Every moment you waste spending
Time on anger, hatred or revenge
Is a moment you could have been wending
Through happiness with a good friend
Feeding anger just leads to a dearth
Of the joy that you have on this earth.

Use your time wisely and you
Will find true contentment in life
Let the good things be what you pursue
And an absence of hatred and strife
Will fill your time with good things
Not the acid that negativity brings

Old Age

Once you have been relegated to the trash heap of old age
No one listens, no one bothers, they avoid you like a plague
It's like you have a disease that they are afraid to get
So they stay away so as not to get caught up in your net

They do not want to listen to your wisdom or your stories
Of how things were when you were young and in your glory
They want to do things their way 'cause
they know so much better
Forgetting you've "been there, done that"
when you were a go-getter

And so old people sit alone and ponder on their fate
Knowing death is waiting patiently just outside the gate
To take you to your resting place and dark eternity
While the young try to ignore their inevitable destiny

Now is the Future

With but a short time left to retirement
What a breeze my life has become
I don't have to meet any requirements
My career ambition is done
I am coasting to a stop and waiting on the end
Looking forward to tomorrow and life's labours dividends

I have spent the last fifty-six years bending to someone's will
Quite soon now the only one to answer to is me
I am sure it will be quite strange for a bit until
I get into the routine of really being free
Then the joy of freedom will well and truly start
I'll spend my time in writing rhymes that
come straight from the heart

Religious Folly

Why is it that god is so divisive
He is supposed to be the symbol of love
Yet there are so many Perceptions of God
Each group is convinced they have the one true answer
And are willing to kill to assert their claim.

More people have been killed in his name
Than any other reason

Don't shave
Don't cut your hair
You must wear a hat
You must pray four times a day facing east
Cows are sacred
God has an elephant's head
Don't eat meat on Fridays

Why does God only speak to certain people
Why do we believe these people
Why is it we have to accept things on blind faith
Why do we credit these things
Anymore than the Tooth Fairy
Santa Claus
The Easter Bunny
They make no more sense

Down the ages religion has been the inspiration
For beauty
Mercy
Learning
Art
Architecture
Laws for Good
Punishment of Evil
Concepts of Right and Wrong.

It has been the cause of Holy Wars
(an oxymoron)
Jihad
Inquisitions
Repression of knowledge
Cruelty and all manner of insanity.

Religion has scaled the heights of imagination
And plumbed the depths of depravity
Religion has practiced liberality
And Oppression
All in the name of the Almighty.

Is it not time to call a halt to the festivities
In this age of enlightenment and knowledge
Should we not know better
Are we not past the point where we need to be led

The spirit of god lies within us all
You just need to know where to look
That little voice that tells you right from wrong
That guilty feeling that won't let you sleep at night
The whisper in your ear when
You are going to take the "easy way"
That says, "Do the right thing"
And when you do it feels so good and right.

You won't get to heaven by following religious dogma
But you will get to heaven by doing the right thing!

Unknown Options

One cannot help but wonder as the sands of time slip by
What would have happened if I'd given that other choice a try
And thus begun a different path to the one I chose
With life unfolding in a manner diverse from my molded prose

The man that missed his morning bus that
crashed further down the line
The girl that went on a blind date that turned out really fine
The boy that in a fit of pique dropped out of school
And thus became a rock star by not following the rules

Small instances of happenstance that form our day to day
Creating the mosaic that occurs along the way
We travel through life's journey from the cradle to the grave
In a completely random manner like a surfer on a wave

To Thine Own Self Be True

People are amazing in every way
Just when you think you've seen it all
Along comes someone with a game to play
And gobsmacks you in a way that can appall
The truth gets lost in the smoke and lies
Creating the Gordian knot that ties.

If we would all just play it straight
Stop dealing cards from up our sleeves
It would relieve most of the weight
Of conflict that we ourselves have weaved
Thus making life a smoother road to travel
With fewer bumps to make it unravel.

Shakespeare said:

"TO THINE OWN SELF BE TRUE, AND IT SHALL FOLLOW AS THE NIGHT THE DAY, THAT THOU CANST NE'ER BE FALSE TO ANY MAN"

Time is the Cure

The winds of change are blowing through the trees
Storm clouds are glowering on the horizon's edge
Emotions are unsettled being buffeted in the breeze
It seems that the world is tottering on the ledge
Of disaster, trouble seems to loom at every turn
It appears as if the universe will burn

Take heart, for tomorrow is a new day
These things too shall also pass and fade
They are merely bumps along the way
Another scene in history's continuing parade
The sun will shine on tomorrow's dawn
The fog of yesterday's malaise will soon be gone

Time in Emergency

Sitting in the waiting room of an Urgent Care
Filling in the time it makes you wonder
As the people come and go while you're sitting there
The mishaps and the suffering give you pause to ponder
On the unknown stories unfolding in this place
A snapshot of humanity held within this space

The drunk who fell and broke his arm is waiting for his cast
The boy who fell from his bike and now needs a dressing
The baby with a fever needs some antibiotics fast
A woman suffering from abuse could use a counselor's blessing
They are all here sitting and waiting in this space
Hoping against hope that they're the next one in place

They are the sad and luckless of Fate's happenstance
Brought together by the turning of life's wheel
If not for the impersonal randomness of chance
They'd be elsewhere and enjoying how they feel
But by luck they're waiting, sitting in this place
Bored, uninterested and staring off blankly into space

Soon this will pass into the scrapbook of their time
Just another anecdote for them to relate
To a group of friends in a much happier clime
When things are not as addled as on this date
In a far warmer and a cozier place
Surrounded by a group of friends, a more conducive space

The Human Condition

We are all together in this world for better or for worse
Thus it makes more sense to go along to get along
Why waste time butting heads when the only real recourse
Is being respectful of the other even if you think they're wrong

History has proved that an idea cannot be suppressed
You can't change someone's mind through a loud voice
Persuasion is the only way for you to impress
Your ideas on them and let them make their choice

Everyone will not agree on any given thing
Compromise is the only way to get through
Give and take is the only way that you can bring
About consensus on any problem that is facing you

Waste not time on looking back on past battles lost
Look at what is here right now and what you can do
To advance the situation and hence reduce the cost
To everyone involved so that success will win through

The Great Leveller

The fog filters down between the stones
It's grey white tendrils caressing each name
Quietly, impervious the lingering bones
Ignore the intrusion of nature's game.

The names of the long forgotten who lay here
Remembered by none but the grounds keeping crew
Who knew them not in life, but now are near
Them daily as they have their duties to do.

Death is the great leveller of us all
We all end the same, anonymous here
It matters not whether great or small
Time erases memory year by year.

Em Ge

There once was a girl, Macy by name
Who, to her lasting fame
Spread goodness and kindness
That never was mindless
But an intricate part of her game.

But there was another side to her face
Which she wielded with aplomb and grace
A certain flare for sass
Applied with some class
To put unkind people in their place.

Appreciation

In our daily lives we should stop and ponder
On what we have, and the way
That the ones who created the wonder
That we call our world today.
If not for their efforts to advance the way we live
We would not be as we are and all that has to give.

Sir Isaac Newton said:

"THE ONLY REASON WE CAN SEE SO FAR TODAY, IS BECAUSE WE ARE STANDING ON THE SHOULDERS OF GIANTS"

Pearls of wisdom at the feet of the Master

CHAPTER FIVE
A Fresh Start

A Fresh Start

A brand new city and a brand new start
New worlds to conquer, a new job to do
Looking forward with an open heart
To a life with a brand new view

Shake the dust of the past off my feet
Old wrongs, old hurts matter not a whit
Smile and shrug and prepare to greet
Tomorrow, and that's the truth of it

You cannot undo the past, it's true
Don't let it intrude and get in the way
Of the success in what is awaiting you
On this much brighter and sunnier day

Above and Beyond

Three years ago my wife hired a personal companion
Who turned out to be an angel in disguise
This girl then recruited another who was also a champion
Of efficiency and kindness, reliable and wise.

Last year my wife was involved in unfortunate mishap
Which landed her in the hospital for a spell
This pair of caring people stepped up and filled the gap
Of things not provided by the system very well.

Once out of the hospital they continued with their aid
Going above and beyond anything required
They are friendly and warm and can handle any task that's laid
On them, gladly and do what is desired.

Oh blessed is the fate that sent Joey and Macy our way
They are treasures and are quite above compare
I dread the day when they move on to practice in their trade
And am thankful for every day they're here.

The Changing Seasons

The wind is whipping the trees and rain
Leaves are scattered and carelessly strewn
Into windrows only to be driven again
When the next gusts come bursting through.

Late autumn and the weather glowers
Saddening the heart and the spirit cowers
Soon winter's hoar frost will rime the earth
Long dark nights with warmth a dearth.

The Ides of March and winter's slow retreat
As the days lengthen and the earth slowly warms
Jack Frost leaves on dragging feet
Then fresh green starts to be the norm.

Spring turns to summer, all is laughter and fun
The days are long and full of sun
September comes and the days draw in
Too soon the fall rains start to begin.

Life is a sine curve, all highs and lows
Everything changes, good and bad
Triumph and tragedy, that's how it goes
Chin up it soon passes, smile and be glad.

Second Childhood

Over the years of our marriage
My wife has often said to me
Why don't you act your age
Stop acting so childish and silly.

At the ripe old age of seventy-one
It really seems to me
I deserve to have some fun
Whatever that may be.

As long as no one gets harmed
By the jokes or the pranks that I pull
Then it's one of the charms
Of living life to the full.

When my second childhood arrives
I should be in great form
Since I've been practicing all my life
My childhood is the norm.

So I guess the answer is then
I am truly acting my age
Since for sixty odd years I've been ten
I have never gone past that stage.

Random Thoughts

In that twilight zone 'twixt wake and sleep
The mind just wanders randomly
Thoughts pop up as the subconscious creeps
Into a world of fantasy

What would have happened if I went left not right
Where would I be now, today
I would have met different circumstances that might
Have changed my life in a drastic way

The mind plays tricks and reality blurs
Into the dream world of fantasy
Bearing no resemblance to what occurs
In your normal day to day

When you awake and sleep's fog is done
It's hard to remember the jumbled tale
That flashed through your mind and now it's gone
Into the past like a lost e-mail

Fantasy Land

Alternate facts make the truth change
Truth and lies become quite blurred
Said loud and often they re-arrange
The events that have occurred

So it seems that fact is fiction
Making fiction into fact
So with Donald's predilections
Of saying what is not exact

Anything that runs contrary
To his egotistical bent
Never letting the story vary
From himself magnificent

Those who point to his failings
Are liars, deceitful, and a blight
His tweets are the inane wailings
Of things in his narcissistic light.

So it would seem that we behold
Cartoon characters now run the place
Donald and Mickey now unfold
A government that's a true disgrace

January 1st 2017

2016 has faded into the dust of the past
2017 stretches out into the future's mist ahead
Real time, with the media's help, moves so fast
Events, like grapeshot, rattle round in our head
One never knows what tomorrow may bring
Whether strange new worlds or the same old thing

It seems there's nothing new under the sun
Governments rise and fall and factions war
The world turns and things continue ever on
Fame comes and goes, the public snores
Through the night, oblivious to it all
Inured to the mayhem outside their walls

Will this year be different, logic says no
Chaos is rampant, mayhem ensues without end
Violence breeds violence, to what end no one knows
If the world could take pause, if just for a second
Perhaps breaking the cycle of endless strife
Causing mercy and peace to take on a new life

Religion is the most divisive of things
Segregating people in groups, each one intending
To encompass the world with one true offering
Of how God bestows on we humans his blessing
When in truth it's all about money and power
Whatever sells best to the most in that hour

God isn't in Mecca or Calcutta or Rome
He resides in the heart, an emotional space
Let goodness and mercy find a permanent home
In your life and you'll find the glow of his grace
May 2017 bring us all happiness and peace
Let the anger and strife gradually cease

"What fools are we who cannot see The forest for the trees"

Once you have been relegated to the realm of stagnation
People start to look at you as something out of time
A fossil of the past who has no inclination
To reach the next rung in ambition's climb

They do not stop and see the world around us
They only see the next prize they want to land
By striving hard for a seat on the success bus
They miss out on the moment in which they stand

Retired people are to be avoided or ignored
They have no place in the normal "day to day"
No one wants to be stuck and bored
By their stories of their other older ways

Perhaps if people listened to what they have to say
They might learn a better way and understand
That being old is to be a victim of time's sway
A situation that occurs quite out of hand

The Future

As the days dwindle down and retirement looms
The future starts to look a scary place
With no job to go to, life looks empty in the gloom
A pointless hollowness is staring you in the face.

It is tough to picture after fifty-six years
Of being in the work force day to day
A blank tomorrow, and now facing the fear
Of no reason to push your footsteps on life's way.

There has to be a reason to get up each morn
Something other than just more of the same
Else there is no point in being born
Just wasting space to your lasting shame.

A sense of achievement drives one ever on
Having a purpose is the dividend
When that the driving force is gone
You are spinning your wheels out to the end.

I must learn to use my rhymes to fill my time
And doing all the things I like to do
Spinning out my days as I did in my prime
Looking at the future as an endless view.

The Eternal Sea

Never resting, moving ever on
The sea rolls constantly in motion
With an energy that is never gone
Forever, ceaselessly in action
The mood and colour always changing
Grey and scowling, blue and mild
Dark and forbidding, rearranging
Sometimes calm and sometimes wild
Alluring and fascinating like an enchanting lover
It draws you in, you're held in thrall
It's an addiction from which you'll ne'er recover
It will haunt your life for ever more.

Democracy's Illusion

People think that they have a say
In the Government's day to day
When the reality is they're merely pawns
In the game of power and the wealth it spawns.

When an election is called, a vote you get
A say in who wins the election bet
And that's as far as your freedom extends
All you can do in the government's trends.

He who pays the piper calls the tune
Excepting the taxpayer who fills the spoon
Of the government coffers, so that they can spend
On government contracts for themselves and their friends

Politicians spout of the public weal
When all they want is the best deal
That which will help them in the next election
Seeming to be the one who is the best selection.

Voter disaffection and ennui in the process
Should tell the government to clean up the mess
But changing the process is beyond their ken
So it all remains the same as way back when.

They all want to get theirs before the gravy stops
And it all collapses as the bottom drops
Out of the lucrative government pay chest
Stopping the tax dollars feathering their nests.

Unfortunately, our system seems to be the best
And that speaks volumes about the rest
Fascism, Communism, republicanism, who cares who wins
As long as it is the party that you happen to be in!

A System Perpetuated

Idealism is a conundrum of great proportion
Since by definition it must be
Perfect in it's symmetrical contortion
Unlike in the real world, imperfectly
An illusion which you can only teach
Just a dream that never can be reached

Lawyers and politicians seem to exist
In an illusory world of make believe
Where everything is possible and consists
Of rules and solutions which they think will relieve
All the problems that in the world abound
We mere mortals must survive what they propound.

Neither of these groups it seems to me
Understand the implications of the ripple effect
Nor can they see the forest for the trees
Going on without a pause to reflect
On the damage or the cost to you and me
Just centered on what they deem should be.

Since most politicians start out in law school
It should be no surprise that they pass
Writs that seem designed so that the rules
Can only be interpreted by their class
Not written in the vernacular of the day
Making it a game that only they can play.

The Government claims that since they were elected
That they are doing what the voter's ask
But Justin Trudeau was only selected
By thirty-nine percent of the people who cast
A vote in the late electional whim
Which means sixty-one percent did not vote for him.
As most of the people did not select
Him, his mandate is not desired
By most of the country who did not elect
The government that is now in charge.
He rules, as did his father once before
On his capricious, idealistic mores.

He will decide, he knows what's best
No matter the cost, we can all afford to pay
After all, he passed the election's test
And so on with the show as day by day
The fiasco continues to the tax payer's cost
What the people want seems to get tossed.

We will have him for five years no matter what
And the truth of it all is it matters not
Since the alternatives were probably no better
Just a different idealistic go-getter.

Sir Winston Churchill said:

"DEMOCRACY IS A TERRIBLE FORM OF GOVERNMENT, BUT IT'S WAY AHEAD OF WHATEVER IS SECOND."

Idealists

There are people who do not live in the real world
They think in terms of a Utopian Society
People who cannot see the forest for the trees
So busy looking at the individual's rights
They lose sight of the big picture

A law that lets a guilty person walk free
Knowing that they are guilty is wrong!
Just because someone skirted the rules
Does not justify freeing a miscreant
Rather we should punish both
The individual who broke the law
And the one who flouted the rules to convict

The truth should be tantamount!

Thinking you can defeat terrorists with kindness
Is to hope water will flow uphill
A person who is willing to kill to gain their ends
Is not capable of understanding reason
You cannot defeat barbarism with kindness
Religious fanaticism is irrational and dangerous
Whether the person actually believes his dogma
Or is using it for personal gain matters not a whit
Each is equally inherently evil
God is not on the side of the righteous
God is on the side of the biggest club
Right only triumphs over wrong
When right has the biggest army

An idealist running a government is a sure calamity
They tend to focus in on a problem
Forgetting all else
And the price of following the particular dream
Foremost in the moment

It is all very well to think it is unfair
For some people to have nothing
While others have lots, taxing them heavily
But why is it fair to take the money from those who earn it
And give it to the people who don't?

Socialism works, so you don't have to
Don't worry the government is paying

Wake up!
The government is NOT paying
YOU ARE
The government has no money
It gets its money from the taxpayer
That's you and me, the average Joe

There is one taxpayer for all levels of government
Be it Civic, Provincial, or Federal
Our Prime Minister seems to think
Taxing the haves more heavily is good
What does he care, he isn't paying
He just bumbles along in his dream world
And we pay for his folly
Again!

At a time when our economy is struggling
He thinks it is kind to take in
An inordinate amount of refugees
And that the average person will be happy
Mortgaging our future and our children's future
So that his dream is possible

Once more living in a dream world
Never having to have worked for a living
Born with a silver spoon in his mouth
He has no concept of the real world
Or the average person's struggle to make ends meet

Raised by an arrogant rich father
Who also was an idealist
Thinking he knew what was best for all
Never mind the consequences

God protect us from well meaning fools!

The American Myth

The United States was founded by groups
Of people seeking freedom
It was not
The United States was founded by people who
Wanted freedom for themselves
And those who thought like them.
The most oppressive regimes were the
Puritans who crushed or ostracized anyone
Who did not conform
So much for personal freedom

The Founding Fathers were slave owners
The Founding Fathers did not believe in universal suffrage
Only the landowners and wealthy could vote
So much for Liberty and Equality for All!

The Founding Fathers rebelled against
What they called unfair taxation by Britain
Then promptly rebelled against their own governments
Who taxed even more heavy handedly than Britain ever did.

To this day United States citizens do all they can to avoid
Government taxation
They want all the amenities
As long as they don't have to pay for it!

The United States history is not one of
Freedom loving peoples
It is one of oppression and conquest.
Slowly eliminating and destroying anything
Or anyone who stood in their way.

First the Indians
Then Mexico
Then the buffalo

"To the Victor goes the spoils"
"History is written by the Victors"

Hence the Great Myth
"Our country was founded by men who
sought personal freedom"
As long as the freedom was theirs.
"A citizen's right to bear arms"
Was written by slave owning Christian white men
Who were concerned
That an Indian or a Redcoat was going to appear.
They also needed their guns to feed themselves

The men who wrote the constitution
Had no concept of the United States
As we know it today

Any law that let's a guilty person go free
IS WRONG

The concept of Manifest Destiny was conceived
By men who did not know what was beyond
The Appalachian Mountains
The Mississippi River had been seen by very few
They had no idea of where the West Coast was
Or how much land and how many people
Lay between them and the west coast

These are the men who called the Indians
To a peace parlay and gave them presents
Of blankets infected with smallpox
Thusly wiping them out and solving the problem

So much for a country founded on personal freedom
As long as it was THEIR personal freedom.

I do not hate the United States
In fact, I feel a certain kinship with them.
Every country's history is full
Of evil deeds and nefarious men and acts
Each is based solely on self-interest.

What I do find insulting is
The way they claim to be the one true way
In the world
Their world.

"Man learns nothing from the past
Each regime succeeds the last
Egyptian, Greek, Roman, British
Who will be there at the finish"
In the musical "Chicago" Richard Gere sings
"Give 'em the old razzle dazzle"
It should be the United States National Anthem

If you doubt this, remember
This is the country that elected George Bush Jr.
TWICE
And Donald Trump is the Presidential Front-runner

Thoughts on Life

The sands of time move by so fast
Unnoticed in the day to day
'Til one day you see that most are past
And life is ebbing rapidly away
Do the things you can before your time is stilled
Ere it all closes down and leaves you unfulfilled.

In youth all is for your tomorrows
Stretching endlessly towards the sun
There's lots of time so you can afford to borrow
Days from your future on your run
Then, sudden, all your tomorrows are spent
Leaving you wondering where they went.
Savour each moment before it's gone
Treat it as if it were your last
Regret only what you have not done
Bite deep into the feast of life's repast
Thusly live life to it's full extent
Leaving you nothing to repent.

Philosophical Moments

Whilst working in the cemetery preparing a spot
For the next customer who recent passed away
It starts one wondering at how much time we've got
'Twixt birth and death, the in between,
our lives from day to day.

It all passes by so quickly, scarce time to take a breath
From youth to middle age in the blinking of an eye
Too soon old age is on you and facing your impending death
Amazed at the speed with which it all went by.

The moral of the story, it seems obvious to me
Is to enjoy what you have while it's in front of you
For soon, as a leaf on a river, this moment will be
Gone, never to return, no matter what you do.

Mortality's shadow hangs heavy on us all
Like footsteps echoing down an empty hall
The constant ticking of life's clock hanging on the wall
One never knows where or when or how the axe will fall.

Live each moment to the fullest before the curtain stays
And you slip into the void of the eternal night
Drink deep of life's cup, waste not a single day
Thus making your life a bright and burning light.

A Blank Page

A new born child, a joyous thing
Beauty and innocence personified
All the promise that hope can bring
Ready for a trip on life's wild ride

The whole of the world is at their feet
And endless opportunities abound
All is new and ready to greet
The brand new life on the merry-go-round

This child may grow to create new science
Literary works that dazzle the mind
Be a strong leader of great reliance
Or amaze the world with new finds

There is also the darker side
Adolf Hitler was once a child
The addict, the prostitute, once did reside
In the cradle a baby mild

What sets our feet on the path we tread
How do we drift to left or right
What nudges us to this one instead
Of the other which may lead to the light

A word of encouragement at a given moment
May influence a child's choice
And set their feet toward a talent
They otherwise might not have voiced

A simple hug and a kindly word
Could show the child the world's not all sad
When abuse and anger is all they've heard
Is it any wonder that they turn out bad

In the future when you see a child you should
Give a thought to what you show
Try to influence them toward the good
Making the future better for you both

Demagoguery

In 1920 an unknown, unkept individual
Became member number 555 of a small
Unknown right-wing political party.

The world would later tremble at the sound of his voice
His name was Adolf Hitler

By 1924 he had transformed this motley group
Into a force to be reckoned with
He renamed it
The Nationalist Socialist German Worker's Party
It had nothing to do with socialism
In fact, it was socialism's implacable enemy.

He fed into the fears of a conquered people
He gave the people someone to blame for their ills
He fostered "The stab in the back" rhetoric
He blamed profiteers and socialist
politicians for Germany's defeat
He gave the people a focus for their anger
He said he would make Germany great again.

He slowly removed the opposition by force
He eliminated all other political parties
He tightened his grip until
His was the only voice the people heard.

And then he led his country to total destruction

In the 2016 Presidential Campaign in the United States
There is a candidate who is following a similar path

He promises to make America great again
He attacks groups for people to take out their anger on
The illegal Mexican immigrants, the Muslims,
Anyone who disagrees with him

He wants to limit the press and reporters
He wants to prosecute any hecklers or dissidents
He advocates violence to all who are not his followers

He promises to protect America from all her enemies
He will build walls on America's borders

The truth has no place in his campaigns
He tells whatever the group he is speaking to
Exactly what they want to hear
It doesn't matter whether it is doable or not
His claims are whatever fits the moment

The parallels are patently obvious
The parallels are patently fearful.

Perhaps he will not follow the same path onward
But the outset is decidedly worrisome

Lord Acton said: "Power corrupts, and
absolute power corrupts absolutely"

Is there any reason to believe
That if the candidate does get the nomination
And does get elected to the White House
(Remember, this is the country that elected
George Bush Jr. TWICE)
That he will suddenly become more mellow
That he will be grow into moderation?

Is it possible, absolutely
Is it probable, NO.

There is a Broadway song called "the old razzle dazzle"
This truly describes the particular candidate
And his practices
"How can they hear the truth above the roar"

Perhaps sanity will rule
But I'm not holding my breath.

Not for Ourselves Alone

HMCS Bonaventure, "The Big Bold B"
Was the last aircraft carrier Canada had
She was the pride of the fleet for all to see
And when she was scrapped all were sad
The end of an era, another page turned
One more tradition had been spurned

Canada's Navy had a proud tradition
Rooted in World War Two's convoy system
Through six long years we held our station
Against the best the U-Boats could throw at them
Through shot and shell and endless storms
Hardship and turmoil was the norm

From this birth of fury and of fire
Arose a Navy proud and strong
Giving recruits an example to aspire
An "esprit de corps" for them to belong
"The Big Bold B" became the last
Of that mold to be cast

She was the flagship of the fleet
Showing the flag, far and wide
When Canada went to Cyprus to meet
The civil war crisis from the inside
The "Bonnie" took the troops to the troubled land
To keep the peace, staying war's hand

First, the new flag and the ensign changed
Tri-service was the next in line
A green uniform for all was now exchanged
And tears were shed for the decline
Of the seaman's rig of old
Worn by the veterans strong and bold

Next women came to join the fleet
And political correctness started to appear
"Jolly Jack Tar" was being squeezed
Out of existence, it was clear
That the ribaldry of older days
Would soon be gone into the past's haze

Change is constant in all things
It is neither good nor bad
Yet still nostalgia will bring
A wistful sigh and a heart that's sad
For the passing of a way of life
Traditions that conquered in that strife
Should the call come again, will these
Of the new generation face the dare
Of death and destruction on the seas
Or will they just stand and stare
Careful not to insult or offend
Hoping the enemy will be their friend.

Alternative Facts

Emanating from the Trump Presidency
Is a new term for the modern lexicon
"Alternative Facts" seems to be
The hook to hang his versions on
To the average person this means obfuscation
To cover Mr. Trump's insecurity and fiction

He thinks that he can say anything
Not letting the facts get in the way
That saying it loud and often will bring
About a new truth to carry the day
His reality seems to be in a zone
Inhabited by him and the faithful alone

How insecure and fragile is he
To overcompensate in such a way
A megalomaniac for all to see
"Alternative Facts" to explain away
Anything that he thinks detracts
Regardless of the actual facts

His ridiculous statements boggle and stun
Reality holds no brief with him
All that counts is that he's the one
All must cater to his whim
He is the greatest and the best
Miles ahead of all the rest

There is a saying that goes:

"IF YOU HAVE TO TELL PEOPLE HOW GOOD YOU ARE, CHANCES ARE YOU AIN'T"

Revolution

Status Quo breeds complacency
Nobody cares
Preferring consistency
Nobody dares
To take serious action
Against the tide
Of incompetence and corruption
On every side
'Til comes the last straw
Breaking the camel's back
No time to withdraw
No turning back
Chaos flares
When the order's replaced
And no one is there
To fill in the space
The vacuum will fill
Very quickly indeed
Do what you will
Events will proceed
So be sure that you're ready
To provide a new hand
That is better
Than the old one's last stand
Change is only a good plan
If what you apply
Is much better than
What the old one tried
So before you decide
To tear out the old
Be sure to provide

Something good to behold
Lest you find what you've wrought
Is not any better all told
It all went for naught

A Good Deeds Reward

Born into a life of poverty and need
Never knowing anything but a dearth
A life spent struggling to feed
One's self or getting anything of worth.

A childhood spent in hunger and a lack
Of anything that makes life an easy place
Forces people into taking a tack
They otherwise might not have had to face.

If given half a chance they could become
A functioning member of society
But given the environment they are from
Breaking free is not too likely.

With no hope of ever breaking out
They fall into a cycle of degradation
Leaving their chances of a future in much doubt
Of anything except more desperation.

In the future let us all do what we can
To try to steer the young one's hearts and minds
Toward a bright tomorrow with a helping hand
Getting them to the front, not from behind.

We will all get a blessing from the act
Your life, and theirs will be the better for it
Their lives won't be a waste and that's a fact
Society and everyone will profit from it.

Subsumption

Mankind's history is one long story of struggle
As societies constantly continue to juggle
For positions of dominance on the world's stage
Endlessly contending throughout each age.

As each one rose to a dominant place
It got there by taking its neighbour's space
Subsuming them into the greater whole
Morphing them into a subservient role.

Once absorbed into the greater whole
The subsumed group's traditions and roles
Subtly changing the society's face
Making the whole a better place.

Society is constantly morphing and changing
Endlessly moving and rearranging
New groups rise as the old ones fall
Not always to the betterment of all.

'Tis the law of the jungle, the strong survive
The weak and the slow are eaten alive
God's not on the side of the right
The winner is the one with the most might.

Man learns nothing from the past
Each regime succeeds the last
Egyptian, Greek, Roman, British
Who will be there at the finish?

"Those who do not learn history are doomed to repeat it"
George Santayana

Personal Priorities

Sometimes in life there comes a personal epiphany
From quiet contemplation on a personal review
A sudden blinding light on the relevancy
Of what you thought important, but it is only to you
Others do not see it as important to them in the end
They have priorities of their own with which to contend

When taken in context, your importance is not tantamount
For others there are more immediate things
That overshadow that which you thought was paramount
And is really so much less so in the order that life brings
That which you find devastating and the end of days
Others do not feel the urgency in the swing and sway

It is difficult to find you are not as important as you thought
To others you are just a little further down the scale
Try to see the other side and not get caught
In self-absorption and the misery that that entails
Instead be helpful to the others in their hour of need
Understanding and kindness are a far worthier deed

If each of us could be a little more considerate of the rest
Not being so self-absorbed, try to see the others need
Understanding where they are coming from is best
Getting a view of their side is a kinder creed
If we all could only be just a little more generous
The world would be a much better place for all of us

The Fading Light

For the last month or so I'm feeling that the end is near
(My seventy-second birthday is but six weeks away)
I am feeling the necessity of all the things that I hold dear
Had better not be deferred for another day

I must complete my tasks before the end arrives
Lest all the undone things are lost and not survive

I have no fear or dread about my impending end
The inevitability of it is a given verity
But I feel a sense of urgency about the
things I want to transcend
My sloughing off this mortal coil and leave to posterity

I suppose that in reality it will never be totally done
Until Atropos cuts the thread and my race is run

I'd like to think that when death comes I'll meet it with a bow
And slip gracefully into my eternal rest
I know that I will rest easier because my rhymes will flow
On into the future, thus surviving time's test

Achieving a small slice of immortality
Will be very satisfying and rewarding for me.

The Fullness of Life

The cat's paws pad silently by
Just like time they're on the fly
Let not a candle pass unburned
Wasted time does not return

Do all you might with what you have
All to soon arrives the grave
If not struck at as it's swung
The bell will forever stay unrung

Enjoy each moment to the full
Soon old age will start to pull
Down proud youth until at last
You'll find your tomorrows are all past